Beyond Belief

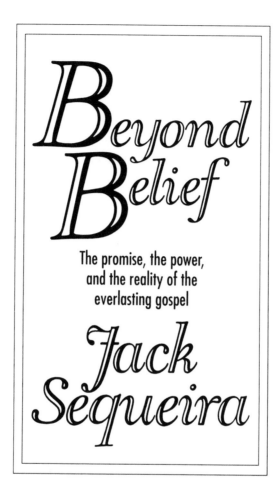

Beyond Belief

The promise, the power,
and the reality of the
everlasting gospel

Jack Sequeira

Pacific Press Publishing Association
Boise, Idaho
Oshawa, Ontario, Canada

Edited by Jerry D. Thomas
Designed by Tim Larson
Typeset in 11/13 Century Schoolbook

Library of Congress Cataloging-in-Publication Data:
Sequeira, Jack.
    Beyond belief: the promise, the power, and the reality of the
everlasting gospel / Jack Sequeira.
      p.   cm.
   ISBN 0-8163-1143-9
   1. Salvation. 2. Seventh-day Adventists—Doctrines.
3. Adventists—Doctrines. II. Title.
BT751.2.S325   1993
234—dc20   92-42602
                                           CIP

94 95 96 97 ● 5 4

Contents

Preface

This book presents what I consider to be Scripture's essential teaching about the gospel. Seventh-day Adventists have emphasized the three angels' messages, the very heart of which is "the everlasting gospel" to be proclaimed "to every nation, and kindred, and tongue, and people" (Revelation 14:6). But before we can proclaim this gospel, we must understand clearly what it is—its promise and its power. The implications of this gospel are almost beyond belief, both in the measure of God's love and in His ability to change us. Yet it must become a living reality in our lives.

Jesus said, "This gospel of the kingdom shall be preached in all the world for a witness [a demonstration, see 1 Corinthians 4:20] unto all nations; and then shall the end come" (Matthew 24:14). Yet after almost two thousand years, we must confess that God's people have miserably failed to demonstrate the gospel—this mighty power revealed in Jesus Christ that can deliver us completely from the tyranny of sin and self. We live in the "perilous times" Paul predicted for the last days. Men and women have become "lovers of their own selves . . . having a form of godliness, but denying the power thereof" (2 Timothy 3:2, 5). The church today desperately needs revival (a renewed appreciation of truth) and reformation (a change of behavior). The starting point must be a clear understanding of Jesus and His gospel. This alone will bring sincere repentance and in turn open the way for the Holy Spirit to be poured out as at Pentecost.

This book presents the plan of salvation in a new light and, therefore, will require the reader to put aside all preconceived ideas in order to appreciate its message. As Jesus declared to the disciples of John the Baptist, new wine cannot be put into old bottles (see Matthew 9:17).

For four hundred years, Protestant Christianity has been divided into two camps regarding salvation. The first, Calvinism, confesses that Christ actually saved human beings on the cross, but that this salvation is limited only to the elect—those whom God has predetermined to be saved. The second view, Arminianism, holds that on the cross Christ obtained salvation for all humanity, but that this salvation is only a provision; a person must believe and repent for the provision to become a reality. Both these views are only conditional good news.

I believe that neither camp presents the full truth about salvation. I believe the Bible teaches that God actually and unconditionally saved all humanity at the cross so that we are justified and reconciled to God by that act (see Romans 5:10, 18; 2 Corinthians 5:18, 19). I believe that the only reason anyone will be lost is because he or she willfully and persistently rejects God's gift of salvation in Christ (see John 3:18, 36). This is what constitutes the three angels' messages of Revelation 14, the everlasting gospel that must be preached to every nation, kindred, tongue, and people before the end comes.

That is the purpose of this book.

This book is not for the casual reader. It is not designed to be read so much as studied. Its full value will come as you study it alongside the Bible. As you read each chapter, turn to the texts that are cited; read them for yourself—in more than one translation, if possible. Then the truth as it is in Jesus will come to you directly from God's Word.

In studying the truth of the gospel, you will discover much that contradicts human reasoning. This is because God's Word is not a philosophy but a divine revelation. Reason is important, but we must never substitute reason for revelation. Consider the following texts:

- Isaiah 55:8, 9. God's ways and thoughts are far removed from our ways and thoughts.
- 1 Corinthians 1:17, 18. The gospel, like the cross, is foolishness to the natural mind.
- John 16:12, 13. The Holy Spirit, not our unaided reason, must guide us into truth.

Also, the gospel contradicts our human reason because we are all sinners and continue to fall short of God's glory (see

Romans 3:23). Because of Adam's fall, all humanity is in slavery to sin and hopelessly lost apart from God's saving grace in Jesus Christ. That is why the natural mind can never receive divine truth without the convicting work of the Holy Spirit (see 1 Corinthians 2:14).

I claim no originality for the ideas given in this book. I have tried to present what God has graciously revealed to me through my own study of the Word and through the writings of Spirit-filled individuals past and present. All truth comes from God, and He reveals it in various ways to different persons for the benefit of the total body of Christ.

To all who love the Lord dearly, I send out this book with the earnest prayer that "ye shall know the truth, and the truth shall make you free" (John 8:32).

Chapter One

The Sin Problem

The gospel is God's solution to the sin problem. So it is important to begin our study of the gospel by first understanding sin. Too often we try to understand the solution God has prepared for us in Christ (the gospel) without first recognizing the full extent of the problem (sin). But that is to put matters backward. Only when we truly understand our complete sinfulness in both nature and action will we truly understand God's solution. Not until we understand the depraved nature of sin will we lose all confidence in self and turn to Christ as our only righteousness. The gospel becomes meaningful, then, only against the background of a full understanding of sin.

The origin of sin

Sin originated in heaven in the mind of Lucifer, the leader of the angels (see Ezekiel 28:14, 15). The Bible doesn't explain how sin could arise in a perfect being, because sin is unexplainable. That is why it is referred to as the "mystery of iniquity" (2 Thessalonians 2:7).

The essence of Lucifer's sin was self-exaltation (see Isaiah 14:12-14). Self-centeredness, the love of self, is the underlying principle of all sin. It is in complete opposition to the principle of selfless, self-sacrificing love, which is the foundation of God's character and government (see 1 John 4:7, 8, 16). Sin, then, is

11

basically rebellion against God and His self-sacrificing love.

Lucifer's sin eventually led to open warfare in heaven. He and the angels who sided with him were defeated and cast out of heaven (see Revelation 12:7-9). Although sin originated in heaven in the mind of Lucifer, God did not allow it to develop in heaven. It was here on earth that Lucifer and his angels developed the principle of sin after they were expelled from heaven. Let's see how it happened.

The development of sin

God created this earth for man and gave him dominion over it. All was perfect; sin did not exist in anything that God created (see Genesis 1:26, 28, 31). Sin came into God's perfect world through Lucifer, turned Satan. He tempted our first parents, Adam and Eve, to sin and caused them to fall from the perfect state in which God had created them (see Genesis 3:1-24; Luke 4:5, 6). Thus Satan took possession of this world and made it his own on the basis of the principle "of whom a man is overcome, of the same is he brought in bondage" (2 Peter 2:19).

In the wilderness of temptation, Satan told Jesus that the authority and splendor of the world "is delivered unto me; and to whomsoever I will I give it" (Luke 4:6). Notice that Jesus did not dispute Satan's claim. Since the fall of Adam and Eve, Satan has been the "prince of this world" (John 14:30). In fact, Paul calls him the "god of this world" (2 Corinthians 4:4). As descendants of Adam and Eve, we are in slavery to sin and Satan (see John 8:34; Romans 6:17; 2 Peter 2:19). We are born self-centered, and our natural inclination is to want to live independently of God (see Romans 1:20-23). The whole world is under Satan's control except for those who have given themselves to Christ (see 1 John 5:19).

Using fallen human beings as his tools, Satan has developed a kingdom that is based entirely on self-seeking; the Bible refers to it as "the kingdoms of this world" (Revelation 11:15). It is in complete opposition to God's "kingdom of heaven" (Matthew 3:2), which is based on self-sacrificing love. Everything that goes to make up this world system—politics, education, commerce, recreation, sports, social clubs, technology, nationalism—is founded on Satan's principle of self-love. At times this principle may not be obvious in the things we see around us, but "all that is in the world . . . is not of the Father, but is of the world" (1 John 2:16). Without exception, all that is in the world is based upon "lust," or the principle of self-love.

Because Satan is a liar and a deceiver, much that is in the world appears to be good. But at the end of the world Satan will be completely exposed, and all will see that he has deceived the entire world—both those elements that are obviously evil and those that appear to be good (see Revelation 12:9; 13:3, 4). All that is in the world is part of Satan's kingdom of self-love. For some six thousand years, God has allowed Satan to have his way in developing sin on the earth. But the time will come when Satan and his kingdom will be exposed and destroyed forever (see 2 Peter 3:10-13; Psalm 92:7-9).

Satan and his kingdom must be destroyed, but God has made a way of escape for the fallen human race held captive by Satan (see 2 Peter 3:9). This is the good news, the gospel, that God wants everyone to understand and receive. From the foundation of the world, He has prepared His heavenly kingdom for us (see Matthew 25:34); the destroying fires of hell are intended only "for the devil and his angels" (verse 41). "For God so loved the world, that he gave his only begotten Son, that whosoever believeth in him should not perish, but have everlasting life" (John 3:16). All those who respond in faith to God's love, manifested in the gift of His Son, will be delivered from the condemnation that is resting on Satan and his kingdom (see Romans 8:1; John 5:24).

Sin defined

The Bible uses some twelve different Hebrew words in the Old Testament to define sin and about five Greek words in the New Testament. These can be combined into three basic concepts. All three are expressed in Psalm 51:2, 3: "Wash me throughly from mine *iniquity*, and cleanse me from my *sin*. For I acknowledge my *transgression*: and my sin is ever before me" (emphasis supplied).

Iniquity. The root meaning of this word is "crooked" or "bent." Scripture uses it to describe our natural spiritual condition. The term *iniquity* does not primarily refer to an act of sin but to a condition of sinfulness. As a result of the Fall, men and women are by nature spiritually "bent." Love of self is the driving force of our natures. Paul defines this as "the law of sin and death" that is at work in our lives (Romans 8:2; cf. 7:23). It is this condition that underlies all our sinning and makes us slaves to sin (see Romans 3:9-12; 7:14). The following texts describe our spiritually bent condition:

Psalm 51:5. "Behold, I was shapen in iniquity; and in sin did my mother conceive me." Since David was physically handsome (see 1 Samuel 16:12), he is speaking here of his spiritual condition. From his very conception and birth, he was shaped in iniquity. We are born with a nature that is bent toward sin or self.

Isaiah 53:6. "All we like sheep have gone astray; we have turned every one to his own way; and the Lord hath laid on him the iniquity of us all." This verse makes two points. First, everyone of us has gone astray because we have all followed the natural bent to our "own way." Second, this bent to follow our own way, this self-centeredness, is the iniquity that was laid upon Christ, our Sin Bearer. When He "condemned sin in the flesh" on the cross (Romans 8:3), it was this bent to sin that He condemned. Hence, in spite of our sinful state, there is "no condemnation to them which are in Christ Jesus" (Romans 8:1).

Isaiah 64:6. "But we are all as an unclean thing, and all our righteousnesses are as filthy rags; and we do all fade as a leaf; and our iniquities, like the wind, have taken us away." Because we are "shapen in iniquity" (Psalm 51:5), all the righteousness we produce through our own efforts is like a filthy rag before God; it is polluted with self-love. In contrast to the filthy garments of our own self-righteousness (see Zechariah 3:3, 4), Christ offers us the white robe of His righteousness so that we may be truly clothed and that "the shame of [our] nakedness [does] not appear" (Revelation 3:18).

Matthew 7:22, 23. "Many will say to me in that day, Lord, Lord, have we not prophesied in thy name? and in thy name have cast out devils? and in thy name done many wonderful works? And then I will profess unto them, I never knew you: depart from me, ye that work iniquity." The judgment will expose as iniquity our self-righteous acts—even those done in the name of Christ. Jesus will clearly identify such works motivated by self-love as works of iniquity. Do our works originate from Christ and therefore spring from the motive of self-sacrificing love? Or do they originate from self as a "fair shew in the flesh" (Galatians 6:12)? Are they works of faith, the result of a genuine relationship with Christ? Or are we working in His name without really knowing Him?

Once we understand all that is involved in iniquity, we will realize that nothing good dwells in us (see Romans 7:18). We will then begin to hunger and thirst after the righteousness of Christ offered to us so freely in the gospel.

Iniquity, therefore, is simply the desire to seek our own way. We are born with this bent. It is this condition that makes it impossible for us, apart from a Saviour, to be genuinely righteous, because God's law requires even our motives to be pure and unselfish (see Matthew 5:20-22, 27, 28).

Sin. This is the second term the Bible uses to describe our failures. Its actual meaning is "to miss the mark." Spiritually, this means falling "short of the glory of God" (Romans 3:23) or failing to measure up to His ideal of selfless love.

Since we are all born spiritually bent, it isn't difficult to see why "there is none righteous, no not one," and why "there is none that doeth good, no not one" (Romans 3:10, 12). Our sinful condition (iniquity) makes it impossible for us to do anything but miss the divine mark (sin) unless we have a Saviour. That is why the gospel is our only hope of salvation. Although we have a free will to choose to accept Christ's righteousness or to reject it, we do not have a choice whether to sin or to be righteous. We are born in slavery to sin, and no matter how hard we try or how much we will to do right, we will fall short of the divine mark (see Romans 7:15-24). For further study on this point, read Job 15:14-16; Psalm 14:2, 3; Isaiah 1:4-6; Jeremiah 17:9; and Mark 7:23.

Transgression. This word means a deliberate violation of law, a willful act of disobedience. It presupposes that we have a knowledge of what the law requires. In the spiritual realm, transgression is the deliberate violation of God's moral law, which is His measuring stick for righteousness (see 1 John 3:4). It is knowing God's law that turns sin (missing the mark) into transgression (deliberate disobedience). Note the following texts.

Galatians 3:19. The law was given to make sin into transgression.

James 2:9. The law convinces us that we are transgressors.

Romans 3:20. Through the law we have knowledge of sin.

Romans 5:20. The law did not solve the sin problem, but made it "abound" all the more.

Romans 7:7-13. The law exposes our sinful condition and reveals our total bankruptcy as far as righteousness is concerned.

Since sin is a deceiver, it is impossible for us in our sins to fully realize our condition unless God reveals it to us. This is what He has done by giving the law. He never intended the law to be a means of salvation or for it to deal with sin. Because of our sinful condition, the law cannot produce righteousness in us (see Romans 8:3). We are sold under sin, and the only way we can be saved is in Christ. "By the deeds of the law there shall no flesh be justified in his sight" (Romans 3:20; cf. Galatians 2:16; 3:21, 22; 5:4). God gave the law to us in our sins to be "our schoolmaster [or escort] to bring us unto Christ, that we might be justified by faith" (Galatians 3:24).

That justification by faith will be the subject of the following chapters.

Key Points in Chapter 1
The Sin Problem

1. Sin originated in heaven in the mind of Lucifer, the leader of the angels (see Ezekiel 28:14, 15).
2. Through tempting Adam and Eve into sin, Lucifer (Satan) took possession of this world (see Genesis 3:1-24; Luke 4:5, 6; 2 Peter 2:19).
3. As descendants of Adam and Eve, we are all in slavery to sin. We are born self-centered, and our natural inclination is to want to live independently of God (see John 8:34; Romans 1:20-23; 6:17).
4. The Bible defines sin in terms of three words or concepts:
    a. *Iniquity.* This does not primarily refer to an act of sin, but to a condition of sinfulness; by nature, we are spiritually "bent" (see Psalm 51:5; Isaiah 53:6; Isaiah 64:6).
    b. *Sin.* Literally, "to miss the mark." This refers to our failures to measure up to God's ideal (see Romans 3:23; 7:15-24; Isaiah 1:4-6).
    c. *Transgression.* This is a deliberate violation of God's law, a willful act of disobedience (see 1 John 3:4; Romans 7:7-13).
5. God gave His law to reveal to us our sinful condition. He never intended for the law to be a means of salvation or for it to deal with sin (see Romans 3:20; Galatians 2:16; 3:21, 22; 5:4).
6. The law is to bring us to Christ so that we can be justified by faith (see Galatians 3:24).

Chapter Two

God's Redemptive Love

When the Bible says that "God is love" (1 John 4:8, 16), it doesn't mean that one of His attributes is love. It means that He *is* love. It means that love is the essence of His nature. Because of this, we need to understand everything about God and all that He does in the context of this love. Even His law and His wrath must be understood in the context of His love (see Matthew 22:36-40; Romans 1:18-32). Paul defines God's wrath passively as a love that will not coerce, but allows us to go when we deliberately choose our own way (see Romans 1:24, 26, 28).

We must understand, as well, that the basis of our salvation is also found in God's nature of love. Apart from this love there would be no gospel, no good news (see John 3:16; Ephesians 2:4-7; Titus 3:3-5; 1 John 4:9). Therefore, if we are going to understand and appreciate the good news of our salvation, we must be rooted and grounded in God's love (see Ephesians 3:14-19).

Paradoxically, the greatest stumbling block we have to understanding God's love is our own human love. Most of us make the mistake of projecting human ideals of love on God. We reduce God's love to a human level, thus misrepresenting Him and distorting the gospel of His saving grace in Christ. That is why Paul urges us to understand "the love of Christ, which passeth knowledge" (Ephesians 3:19).

Our modern languages aggravate this problem of understanding God's love. English, like most modern languages, has only a single word for love. This makes it very difficult, when we read of God's love in our English Bibles, to understand the full range of meaning; it makes it difficult to distinguish between God's love and our human concepts of love, all of which are polluted with self. God's love (*agape*) completely contradicts human love (*philos*). We cannot compare the two, only contrast them (see Isaiah 55:8, 9; Matthew 5:43-48; John 13:34, 35; Romans 5:6-8).

Agape and *philos*

The New Testament writers had four Greek words to choose from when describing divine and human love. These four are:

Storge. This is family love or love for one's own kin.

Philos. Affectionate love between two people; brotherly love.

Eros. The common meaning of this word is love between the sexes. We get the English word *erotic* from this Greek word. However, the philosopher Plato gave it a noble, spiritual meaning. He called it "heavenly eros" and defined it as being detached from sensual or materialistic interests to seek after God. Thus, for the Greeks, *eros* as defined by Plato became the highest form of human love. We still speak today of "platonic love."

Agape. This is pure love untainted by any selfish motive whatsoever. In the noun form, it was an obscure word in Greek, an unusual word—perhaps because such love itself is unusual.

The New Testament writers wrote in Greek, so they had these four words to choose from in order to distinguish God's love from human love—or even to distinguish between different types of human love. And they did. The word most commonly used in the New Testament to describe human love is *philos*. (The word *eros* does not appear in the New Testament at all.) And all the New Testament writers chose the infrequently used word *agape* to define God's love.* They took this word and infused it with new meaning based on the revelation of God's love that they saw demonstrated in the life and history of Jesus Christ—and which He displayed supremely on the cross (see Romans 5:6-10). As used by the New Testament

---

*The New Testament does use *philos* at times to describe God's love, but always in the context of *agape*.

writers, this divine *agape* love of God stands in complete contradiction to human love in at least three ways.

1. Human love, either *philos* or Plato's "heavenly eros," is always conditional. As humans, we do not love the unlovely. We love those who love us, who respond to our love. God's *agape* love, on the other hand, is unconditional. It flows from Him spontaneously, without cause, independently of our goodness or self-worth. When we understand this, God's salvation becomes unconditional good news (see Romans 5:6-10; Ephesians 2:4-6; Titus 3:3-5). This is why the Bible so clearly stresses that we are saved by grace alone—God's undeserved, unmerited favor (see Acts 15:11; Romans 3:24; 5:15; 11:6; Ephesians 1:7; 2:8, 9; Titus 1:14; 2:11; 3:7).

2. Human love is changeable. It is a love that fluctuates and is unreliable. A good example of this, and also of the way the New Testament writers deliberately used different words for love, is John 21:15-17. Three times in these verses Jesus asks Peter if he loves Him, and three times Peter replies that he does. In our English Bibles it seems that Jesus' questions and Peter's answers are the same each time. But in His first two questions to Peter, Jesus uses *agape*, the love that will never fail. And Peter replies using the word *philos*, human affection. But when Jesus asks Peter the third time if he loves Him, He uses *philos*. It's as if Jesus says, "Peter, is this the only kind of love you have for Me—this unreliable human love?" No wonder Peter becomes upset! But he is now truly converted and has lost all confidence in himself. In humility, he replies, "Lord, thou knowest all things; thou knowest that I love [*phileo*] thee" (verse 17). This changeable, unreliable *philos* is the only kind of love that we human beings can generate in and of ourselves.

In complete contrast, however, God's *agape* love is unchanging. To the unfaithful Jews, God declared, "I have loved thee with an everlasting love" (Jeremiah 31:3). In Paul's classic description of divine love, "[*agape*] never fails" (1 Corinthians 13:8). Jesus demonstrated this beyond all doubt on the cross when, "having loved his own which were in the world, he loved [*agapao*] them unto the end" (John 13:1).

When we realize this unchanging, unchangeable nature of God's love for us, we will become "rooted and grounded in love [*agape*]" (Ephesians 3:17). We will say with Paul,

> Who shall separate us from the love [*agape*] of Christ? . . . For I am persuaded that neither death nor life, nor angels, nor principalities, nor powers, nor things present, nor things to come, nor height, nor depth, nor any other creature, shall be able to separate us from the love [*agape*] of God, which is in Christ Jesus our Lord (Romans 8:35, 38, 39).

3. At its very best, human love is self-seeking. Since we are by nature egocentric, everything we do or think, in and of ourselves, is polluted with self-love or selfishness. Socially, politically, academically, materially, economically, even religiously, we are all slaves to "our own way" (Isaiah 53:6; cf. Philippians 2:21). As we saw in the previous chapter, we are all shaped in "iniquity," that is, we are bent toward self. Consequently, we all, without exception, fall short of God's glory—His *agape* love (see Romans 3:23).

God's love is the exact opposite. It is self-sacrificing, self-giving. That is why Christ did not cling to His equality with the Father, but emptied Himself and became God's slave, obedient even to death on a cross (see Philippians 2:6-8). All during His life on earth, Jesus demonstrated His Father's *agape* love. This is "the glory as of the only begotten of the Father" that the disciples saw in Him (John 1:14). He lived for the benefit of others; He actually became poor for our sakes, that we through His poverty might be rich (see 2 Corinthians 8:9).

There is no self-love in God's love. This love, reproduced in the lives of Christians through the Holy Spirit, is the most powerful witness of the transforming, saving power of the gospel (see John 13:34, 35).

The supreme manifestation of God's self-sacrificing love was demonstrated on the cross when Jesus Christ died the second death for all humanity (see Hebrews 2:9). This second death is the complete cessation of life; it is saying goodbye to life forever. It's obvious that this is the death Jesus submitted to for us, since Christians who are justified in Christ still have to die the first death (the "sleep" death), but will be exempted from the second death (see Revelation 20:6). On the cross, Jesus was willing to be deprived of life forever, not just for three days, so that we could live in His place. Such self-emptying love transformed His disciples. Before the cross, they were dominated by self-interest (see Luke 22:24). After the cross, they were willing to follow Jesus' example in sacrificing themselves for others. In the same way, when we see the self-sacrificing love of Jesus shining from the cross, we too will be transformed (see 2 Corinthians 5:14, 15).

In summary, then, human love is conditional; God's love is unconditional. Our human love is changeable; God's love is changeless. Our human love is self-centered; God's love is self-sacrificing. Not until we recognize this threefold quality of God's *agape* love will the gospel become unconditional good news to us. And not until we become "rooted and grounded" in His *agape* love will we be able to cast out all fear and serve Him with unselfish motives (see 1 John 4:7, 12, 16-18).

Agape and the great controversy

Satan's rebellion against God in heaven was in reality a rebellion against God's *agape* love, which was the principle underlying the law (see Matthew 22:36-40; Romans 13:10; Galatians 5:13, 14). Lucifer found the idea that love (*agape*) "seeketh not her own" (1 Corinthians 13:5) too restrictive. He rebelled and introduced the principle of self-love or *eros* (see Ezekiel 28:15; Isaiah 14:12-14). Ever since his fall, Satan has hated the concept of self-sacrificing love. When God restored this principle to the human race through the preaching of the gospel, Satan naturally fought against it with all his might (see Revelation 12:10-12). The very first thing he attacked in the Christian church was not the Sabbath or the state of the dead. His onslaughts against these truths came later, but he focused first on the concept of God's *agape* love.

After the apostles passed from the scene, the leadership of the Christian church fell into the hands of the church "fathers." Most of these men were of Greek origin, and they felt insulted that the New Testament writers had ignored what they considered to be the highest form of love—Plato's "heavenly *eros*"—in favor of an obscure *agape*. They felt that because the apostles of Jesus were all Jews (with the exception of Luke) they didn't really understand the Greek language and that a correction needed to be made.

Marcion, who died around A.D. 160, was the first to attempt a change. Next Origen, who died in A.D. 254, actually altered John's sublime statement, "God is love [*agape*]," to "God is love [*eros*]." However, the battle didn't end there. It continued until the time of Augustine, bishop of Hippo in North Africa during the fourth century A.D. and one of the great "fathers" of Roman Catholic theology.

Augustine realized how futile it was simply to substitute *eros* for *agape*. Instead, he did something much more clever and dangerous. Using arguments from Greek logic, he combined the concept of *agape* with the idea of *eros* and produced a synthesis which he called, in Latin, *caritas*. (This is the source of our English word *charity*, which is the word the King James Version of the Bible most often uses to translate *agape*.)

Christendom accepted Augustine's formulation, and *caritas* became the key definition of divine and Christian love in Roman Catholic theology. Since Augustine's idea was a mixture of *agape* and *eros*, the gospel became perverted from "Not I, but Christ" (Galatians 2:20) to "I *plus* Christ." This concept of the gospel is still prevalent today. The moment the pure meaning of *agape* was corrupted, the gospel became perverted with self-love, and the Christian church lost its power and plunged into darkness. Not until the Reformation of the sixteenth century, when Luther realized the problem and tried to undo Augustine's synthesis, did the church begin to emerge into the light of the pure gospel once again. Unfortunately, the Christian church today is still, to a large degree, groping in the darkness, trying to understand the true meaning of *agape* and thus of the gospel.

The three gospels

So we see that there are three concepts of love: *eros,* or self-love; *agape,* or self-sacrificing love; and *caritas,* which is a mixture of self-love and self-sacrificing love. Each of these concepts of love has produced its own gospel.

The various religions of the pagans, who are steeped in *eros*, or self-love, are based on a gospel of works. As the Greek philosopher Aristotle wrote: "Salvation is the movement of the creature toward God." Plato likewise believed that God saves only the lovable. The *eros* gospel teaches that human beings must save themselves by pleasing God through sacrifices and good works. This is legalism, or salvation by works. It is the basis of all non-Christian religions.

The gospel based on *caritas* teaches that we must first show through our good works that we want to be saved; then when God sees this evidence, He will meet us halfway and save us. In other words, we must do our best to meet God's ideal, and Christ will make up the difference. The Galatian Christians fell into this trap (see Galatians 3:1-3), and so have many Christians today. The gospel of faith plus works, or justification plus sanctification, is at the heart of Roman Catholic theology. It is a subtle form of legalism.

The gospel of the Scriptures, however, is neither the *eros* gospel nor the *caritas* gospel. In complete contradiction to both, the apostles taught that while we were helpless, ungodly sinners—even "enemies"—God demonstrated His *agape* love toward us through the death of His Son Jesus Christ, and that that death fully reconciled us to Him (see Romans 5:6-10). This is the clear teaching of the New Testament on the gospel (see John 3:16; Ephesians 2:1-6; 1 Timothy 1:15; Titus 3:3-5).The following diagram represents these three competing gospels:

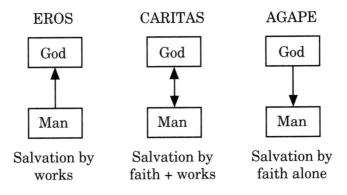

EROS	CARITAS	AGAPE
God	God	God
Man	Man	Man
Salvation by works	Salvation by faith + works	Salvation by faith alone

Both the *eros* gospel and the *caritas* gospel can be described as only conditional good news. Each depends on our fulfilling certain conditions before God extends His grace to us. Only the *agape* gospel is *unconditional* good news, resting solely on God's undeserved favor. That is why this gospel turned the world upside down as the apostles went about proclaiming the glorious message of salvation in Jesus Christ (see Acts 17:6). This is the same gospel that the world so desperately needs to hear today. This is the gospel that will lighten the earth with God's glory before the end comes (see Matthew 24:14; Revelation 14:6-15; 18:1).

Agape and self-worth

One of the effects of sin in our lives is that it tends to produce a sense of low self-worth. Our modern, complex world with its competitive lifestyle has magnified this problem. One result is that those in the counseling business have more work than ever. I don't minimize the value of counseling in certain situations. However, I hope in this book to introduce you to the "wonderful counselor" (Isaiah 9:6) who alone has a permanent solution for low self-esteem.

As we have already seen in chapter 1, the Bible puts little value on our sinful human natures. Jesus said to Nicodemus, whose religion put so much emphasis on human achievement, "That which is born of the flesh is flesh" (John 3:6). By this Jesus meant that our human nature of itself cannot produce anything that God considers good or meritorious (see Romans 7:18). Everything we do, in and of ourselves, is polluted with self-love. That is why there is no one who is good, no one who is righteous, apart from Jesus Christ (see Romans 3:10, 12).

For this reason, Paul warned the Philippian Christians not to have any confidence in the flesh (see Philippians 3:3). Of course, all this is devastating to the human ego. It makes it very hard for us to face ourselves, much less God. The result is a poor self-image, low self-esteem. But the Bible also has good news for us, and that good news is God's unconditional *agape* love. The only permanent solution to the problem of low self-esteem is a clear understanding of God's unconditional love and His saving grace in Jesus Christ. He declares through Isaiah that in spite of our sinfulness, He will make us more precious than the fine gold of Ophir (see Isaiah 13:12). And He has done this in Jesus Christ, as we will see in the next chapter.

Key Points in Chapter 2
God's Redemptive Love

1. Love is not merely one of God's attributes; it is the essence of His nature. God *is* love (see 1 John 4:8, 16).
2. We must understand everything about God—even His law and His wrath—in the context of His love (see Matthew 22:36-40; Romans 1:18-32).
3. The basis of our salvation is found in God's nature of love (see John 3:16; Ephesians 2:4-7; Titus 3:3-5).
4. The New Testament uses the Greek word *agape* to describe God's love. God's *agape* love differs from human love in at least three ways:
   a. Human love is conditional; God's love is unconditional. It flows from Him independently of our goodness or self-worth (see Acts 15:11; Ephesians 1:7; 2:8, 9; Titus 1:14).
   b. Human love is changeable; God's love is unchangeable. His love never fails (see Jeremiah 31:3; Romans 8:35-39; 1 Corinthians 13:8).
   c. Human love is self-seeking; God's love is self-sacrificing (see Philippians 2:6-8).
5. The supreme manifestation of God's unconditional, unchanging, self-sacrificing love was demonstrated when Jesus died the second death on the cross for all humanity (see Romans 5:8; Hebrews 2:9).
6. Three concepts of love have given rise to three concepts of the gospel:
   a. *Salvation by works.* This "gospel" is based on self-love, i.e., human beings must save themselves by pleasing God through good works. This is legalism, and it is the basis of all non-Christian religions.
   b. *Salvation by faith plus works.* This "gospel" is based on a combination of self-love and self-sacrificing love, i.e., we must first show by our good works that we want to be saved—then God will meet us halfway and save us. The "gospel" of faith plus works is at the heart of Roman Catholic theology; it is a subtle form of legalism.
   c. *Salvation by faith alone.* This gospel is based on self-sacrificing love (*agape*); that is, while we were helpless, ungodly sinners, God demonstrated His love for us through

the death of Jesus Christ, and that death fully reconciled us to Him. This is the clear teaching of the New Testament (see John 3:16; Romans 5:6-10; Ephesians 2:1-6; 1 Timothy 1:15).

Chapter Three

The Gospel Defined

In the centuries before Jesus came to earth, the people of Alexandria in North Africa depended for their survival on the wheat brought by grain ships from Phoenicia (present-day Lebanon). It was good news indeed, then, when these ships appeared in port. The Greek-speaking residents of Alexandria actually coined a word to announce the good news that the grain ships had arrived. It is this Greek word that the New Testament uses for the "gospel"—the unconditional good news of salvation for all mankind made sure by the historical reality of Jesus' birth, life, and death (see Mark 16:15; Romans 1:1-14; 10:13-15). The gospel is "good news" indeed.

The apostle Paul calls this gospel "the righteousness of God" (Romans 1:16, 17; 3:21). By this he means that righteousness which God:

1. planned and initiated before the foundation of the world (see Ephesians 1:4; Revelation 13:8);
2. promised since the Fall (see Genesis 3:15); and
3. fulfilled in the life and death of Jesus Christ (see John 3:16, 17; Galatians 4:4, 5).

In other words, it is a righteousness that is entirely of God's doing without any human contribution whatsoever (see Romans

29

3:28; Galatians 2:16). In Christ, according to this gospel, humanity stands perfect and complete before God and His holy law (see Colossians 2:10; Romans 10:4). This salvation delivers us from the three predicaments that we face as sinful human beings. It saves us from:

1. the guilt and punishment of sin.
2. the power and slavery of sin.
3. the nature and presence of sin.

The first salvation is the means of our justification. The second is the means of our sanctification. And the third is the means of our glorification. We need to realize that although we Christians can claim justification as an already-established fact (see Romans 5:1), sanctification is a continuous, ongoing experience (see 1 Thessalonians 4:2-7; 5:23). And glorification is a future hope to be realized at the second coming of Jesus (see Romans 8:24, 25; Philippians 3:20, 21).

All three of these aspects of our salvation—justification, sanctification, and glorification—have already been accomplished in the birth, life, death, and resurrection of our Lord Jesus Christ. Therefore, all three are offered to us in Christ; they cannot be separated. Whom God has justified, He will also sanctify and glorify if we do not turn our backs on Him through unbelief (see Romans 8:30; Hebrews 10:38, 39). All three aspects of salvation make up the gospel—the good news of salvation—and since they come to us in one parcel, Jesus Christ, they are inseparable. We cannot choose to receive one without the others.

Everything we experience in our salvation—either in this world or in the world to come—is based on the finished work of our Lord Jesus. The foundation of all our Christian experience is His birth, life, death, and resurrection. For this reason, we must be grounded in the truth as it is in Him. This is vital, because if our understanding of what Jesus accomplished in His earthly mission is partial or incomplete, so will be our experience. That's why He said, "Ye shall know the truth, and the truth shall make you free." "If the Son therefore shall make you free, ye shall be free indeed" (John 8:32, 36).

Our understanding affects our experience. For example, when

some of the Christians at Corinth denied the resurrection of believers, Paul didn't try to defend the truth of the resurrection by citing proof texts. Instead, he argued that Christians would be raised to life because Jesus had been raised to life (see 1 Corinthians 15:12-23). Likewise, Peter comforted suffering Christians by pointing out that because they were suffering like Christ, they would one day be glorified with Him as well (see 1 Peter 4:13).

Through faith, we identify ourselves with Jesus Christ and His crucifixion. This means that at conversion, when we believe and accept Jesus as our Saviour, we subjectively become one with Him, and His death becomes our death. Faith is being sure of things hoped for (God's salvation in Christ), the substance of which we have not yet fully experienced (see Hebrews 11:1).

The two aspects of salvation

We can divide salvation into two related, but distinct, aspects. First, salvation is what God has already accomplished for all mankind in the life and death of Jesus. This salvation, Jesus said, is the good news, the gospel, and He commissioned His disciples to proclaim it to all the world (see Mark 16:15). Paul often describes this salvation as *you in Christ* (see 1 Corinthians 1:30, 31; Ephesians 1:3-6, 2:13; Philippians 3:9). This salvation is an objective truth realized in the earthly history of Christ, and therefore we can refer to it theologically as *the objective gospel.*

Second, Scripture also refers to salvation as what God accomplishes in us through the Holy Spirit. This aspect of salvation is not something in addition to the objective facts of the gospel. It is making real *in experience* what God has already accomplished for us objectively in Christ. This second phase of salvation may be described, then, as the fruits of the objective gospel. Paul often refers to it by the expression *Christ in you* (see Romans 8:10; Galatians 2:20; Ephesians 3:17; Colossians 1:27). It includes peace with God that comes as a result of justification by faith (see Romans 5:1; Acts 10:36; Colossians 1:20); holiness of living and victory over sin through the process of sanctification by faith (see Romans 6:22; 2 Peter 1:5-7); and the changing of our sinful natures to sinless ones through the glorification to be realized at Christ's second coming (see Romans 8:24, 25; 1 Corinthians 15:51-54; Philippians 3:20, 21). Since this second aspect of salvation has to do with our experience, it is often called *the subjective gospel.*

Today, many Christians are confused about these two aspects of salvation. The confusion comes as a result of failing to see the distinction between what God has already accomplished in Christ some two thousand years ago and what He is presently doing in the lives of believers through the indwelling Spirit. In turn, this confusion has led to much controversy over the doctrine of righteousness by faith. Christ is our righteousness in both of these aspects of salvation; both are made effective by faith alone. But there are important distinctions between the two.

We often describe the first aspect of salvation—the objective gospel—as the *imputed* righteousness of Christ. This is what qualifies the believer for heaven, both now and in the judgment. We describe the second aspect of salvation—the subjective gospel—as the *imparted* righteousness of Christ. This is what gives evidence of the reality of the imputed righteousness of Christ in the life. It does not contribute in the slightest way to our qualification for heaven; it witnesses, or demonstrates, what is already true of us in Christ. Imparted righteousness does not qualify us for heaven, but if it is lacking in our lives, that is evidence that we either do not clearly understand the gospel or that we have rejected the gift of imputed righteousness. A refusal to clothe ourselves with the imputed righteousness of Christ indicates we do not have genuine faith and therefore unfits us for heaven (see James 2:20-23; Matthew 22:11-13).

Differences between "objective" and "subjective" gospels

There are four main differences between the objective gospel ("you in Christ") and the subjective gospel ("Christ in you").

1. *Complete/Incomplete.* Objectively, "in Christ," we stand complete and perfect in all righteousness (see 1 Corinthians 6:11; Ephesians 1:3; Colossians 2:10). Subjectively, "Christ in you" is an ongoing, growing process of sanctification, to be realized before the second coming, and the glorification of our bodies and natures, to be experienced at the second coming (see Romans 5:3-5; 8:18-23; 1 Corinthians 15:51-57; Philippians 3:12-14, 20, 21; Colossians 1:27; 2:6; 1 Thessalonians 5:23, 24; 2 Peter 1:3-8).

2. *Universal/Particular.* "In Christ," all humanity was redeemed—legally justified and reconciled to God (see Romans 5:18;

2 Corinthians 5:18, 19; 1 Timothy 4:10; Titus 2:11; 1 John 2:2).
"Christ in you" applies only to believers who have by faith experienced the new birth (see John 3:16; Romans 8:9, 10; 1 Corinthians 6:17-20; 2 Corinthians 3:17, 18; 6:14-16; 1 Timothy 4:10).

3. *Outside of us/Allied.* "In Christ," the righteousness accomplished is without any help or contribution from us (see Romans 3:21, 28; Philippians 3:9). "Christ in you" involves the cooperation of believers who by faith are walking in the Spirit (see John 15:1-5; 17:23; Romans 8:9-14; 13:12-14; Galatians 2:20; 1 John 3:23, 24).

4. *Meritorious/Demonstrative.* Righteousness "in Christ" is the only means of our salvation, and unless we resist and reject it, it fully qualifies us for heaven both now and in the judgment (see Acts 13:39; Romans 3:28; 10:4; Galatians 2:16; Ephesians 2:8, 9; Titus 3:5). "Christ in you" witnesses to—or gives evidence of—our salvation in Christ, but it is not meritorious (see Matthew 5:14-16; John 13:34, 35; 14:12; Ephesians 2:10; Titus 3:8).

The objective truth of the gospel is that Jesus Christ has already accomplished everything necessary for sinful men and women to be declared righteous and candidates for heaven. Therefore, those who welcome their position in Christ are considered by God as being already righteous, holy, sanctified, and glorified "in Christ" (see Ephesians 1:3-6; 2:5, 6; 1 Corinthians 6:9-11). Luther's great rediscovery that "the just shall live by faith" (Romans 1:17) was the greatest truth to arise in men's minds since the falling away of the gospel in the Dark Ages.

The "in Christ" motif

The central theme of the apostle Paul's theology regarding the gospel is the "in Christ" motif or idea. It is based on the biblical teaching of solidarity or corporate oneness, a concept that is largely foreign to the Western mind although still common in many parts of the world today. The Bible plainly teaches that the whole of humanity is linked together in a common life and therefore constitutes a unit or a shared identity—a corporate oneness.

Notice, for example, how the writer of Hebrews uses this concept of corporate oneness to skillfully weave his argument that Christ's Melchizedec priesthood is superior to the Levitical priesthood (see Hebrews 6:20–7:28). First, he proves that

Melchizedec was superior to Levi. Once he establishes that, it isn't hard to see how Christ's priesthood after the order of Melchizedec is superior to the Levitical priesthood.

But how does the writer of Hebrews prove that Melchizedec is superior to Levi? *Simply by reminding his readers that Levi paid tithes to Melchizedec.* The argument is brilliant; the one who pays tithes is always inferior to the one to whom tithes are paid. But Levi never paid tithes to Melchizedec as an individual! He wasn't even born in the time of Melchizedec. How, then, did he do it? "In Abraham," says the writer of Hebrews.

Levi, Abraham's great-grandson, who had not yet been born, "was yet in the loins" of Abraham (Hebrews 7:10) when Abraham met Melchizedec and paid tithes to him (see verses 7-10). This whole argument is based on the idea of corporate oneness. It helps us understand how all humanity stands condemned "in Adam" and is justified "in Christ," since all humanity were "in the loins" of these two men and were therefore implicated in what they both did.

The Bible view, then, is that God created all mankind in one man, Adam. "And the Lord God formed man of the dust of the ground, and breathed into his nostrils the breath of life" (Genesis 2:7; cf. Acts 17:26). The Hebrew word translated *life* in this verse is in the plural form; it says literally that God breathed into Adam "the breath of *lives*," that is, the lives of all human beings.

In the same way, the Bible considers that when Adam fell, the whole human family fell "in him." Since Adam's sin took place before he had children who could make their own moral decisions, his fall into sin plunged the entire human race into sin (see Romans 5:12; 1 Corinthians 15:21, 22). This view is difficult for the Western mind to grasp and accept because it is much more accustomed to thinking in individualistic terms. However, the idea of all mankind, as a corporate unit, participating in Adam's fall is clearly taught in the Scriptures.

If the downside of the idea of corporate oneness is that we all fell in the one man, Adam, the glorious upside of the idea is that God likewise has redeemed all of us in the one man, Jesus Christ, who is the "second Adam" (see Romans 5:12-21; 1 Corinthians 15:19-23; 45-49). God has legally justified all mankind in Christ just as surely as Satan has brought about the condemnation of all mankind in Adam (see Romans 5:18).

By God's miraculous act, initiated and carried out by Him alone, He united in one person—Jesus Christ—our corporate humanity that needed redeeming with His own perfect divine nature. At His incarnation, Christ assumed the corporate life of the entire human race in its fallen condition (see 1 Corinthians 1:30). Through this mysterious union, God qualified Christ to become the second or "last Adam" (1 Corinthians 15:45). In Hebrew, the word *Adam* means "mankind," and as the second Adam, Jesus Christ became the representative and substitute of corporate humanity. The entire human race is corporately one "in Him" just as we are one "in Adam." What Jesus did, we have done, because we are corporately one in Him. Thus His life and death, which fully met the positive demands of God's holy law as well as its justice, are considered to be our life and death also. "In Him," we are justified because His life and ours were forever linked at the incarnation. This, in brief, is Paul's "in Christ" motif. It is what constitutes the good news of the gospel (see Ephesians 1:3-12; 2:4-7).

Jesus Christ can abide in you through the Holy Spirit (see Romans 8:9, 10) and fulfill in your life the demands of God's holy law (see verse 4) only because of the objective fact that "in Christ" you have already met all the requirements and demands of the law. That is why Paul comes to this conclusion regarding justification by faith: "Do we then make void the law through faith [that is, justification by faith]? God forbid: yea, we establish the law" (Romans 3:31; cf. 10:4).

The idea of corporate oneness—that all humanity was "in Christ"—gives a new understanding to the Bible's teaching of Christ as our Substitute. There is an ethical dilemma in the way we usually think of Christ as our Substitute, a dilemma that is solved by the concept of corporate oneness. That is what we will turn our attention to in the next chapter.

Key Points in Chapter 3
The Gospel Defined

1. In the New Testament, the "gospel" is the unconditional good news of salvation for all mankind made sure by the historical reality of Jesus' birth, life, and death (see Mark 16:15; Romans 1:1-14; 10:13-15).

2. This salvation delivers us from the three predicaments we face as sinful human beings. It saves us from:
   a. the guilt and punishment of sin. This is our justification.
   b. the power and slavery of sin. This is our sanctification.
   c. the nature and presence of sin. This is our glorification.

3. All three of these aspects of salvation—justification, sanctification, and glorification—have already been accomplished in the birth, life, death, and resurrection of Jesus Christ.

4. The apostle Paul describes the salvation God has already accomplished for all humanity in the finished work of Jesus as "you in Christ" (see 1 Corinthians 1:30, 31; Ephesians 1:3-6; 2:13; Philippians 3:9). It can also be referred to as the "objective gospel" because it is an objective truth realized in the earthly history of Jesus.

5. Paul describes the salvation God accomplishes in men and women through the Holy Spirit as "Christ in you" (see Romans 8:10; Galatians 2:20; Ephesians 3:17). It can also be referred to as the "subjective gospel" because it is making real in our experience what God has already accomplished for us objectively in Christ.

6. The objective gospel (the imputed righteousness of Christ) is what qualifies us for heaven—both now and in the judgment.

7. The subjective gospel (the imparted righteousness of Christ) does not contribute to our qualification for heaven; it gives evidence of the reality of Christ's imputed righteousness in the life.

8. The Bible teaches that the whole of humanity is linked together in a common life and therefore makes up a unit or a shared identity—a corporate oneness (see Hebrews 6:20–7:28).

9. The Bible view is that God created all mankind in one man—Adam. When Adam fell, the whole human race fell "in him" because of our shared identity with him. All mankind, as a

corporate unit, participated in Adam's fall (see Romans 5:12; 1 Corinthians 15:21, 22).

10. Likewise, the Bible teaches that God has redeemed all humanity in one man, Jesus Christ, the second Adam (see Romans 5:12-21; 1 Corinthians15:19-23; 45-49).

11. At His incarnation, Jesus assumed the corporate life of the whole human race in its fallen condition (see 1 Corinthians 1:30). The entire human race is corporately one "in Jesus Christ," just as we are one "in Adam." What Jesus did, we have done, because we are corporately one in Him. His perfect life and death are considered to be our life and death as well (see Ephesians 1:3-12; 2:4-7).

12. This "in Christ" motif, based on the biblical teaching of solidarity or corporate oneness, is the central theme of Paul's theology regarding the gospel.

Chapter Four

Christ
Our Substitute

The biblical concept of corporate oneness leads us to the important doctrine of substitution. This doctrine was at the very heart of the theological controversy between the Reformers and the Roman Catholic scholars during the Reformation. The central issue under dispute had to do with the ethical problem raised by the truth of justification by faith. The issue is real, and it still concerns us today: "How can God justify believing sinners and at the same time maintain His integrity to the divine law that justly condemns them to eternal death?" (see Romans 4:5; Galatians 3:10).

The Catholic scholars insisted that before God could declare the individual believer justified, He first had to make him righteous through an infused grace. Otherwise, God is testifying to a lie—declaring a sinner justified who is still a sinner. The Reformers rejected this solution to the problem and came up instead with the biblical doctrine of substitution. "God declares a believer justified," they said, "on the basis of the life and death of Christ, which fully met the law's requirements." In other words, the righteousness of Christ substitutes for the believer's lack of righteousness.

The Catholic scholars would not accept this answer. They argued that such a substitution would be unethical and illegal. No law allows one person to assume the guilt or punishment of another. Righteousness cannot be passed from one person to another. Accordingly, they accused the Reformers of teaching "legal fiction," a "passed-on righteousness," or "celestial bookkeeping."

Both parties were correct to a point—yet both taught error as well. The Catholic theologians were ethically right. God does need to make sinners righteous before He can legally declare them righteous. They were wrong, however, in their solution and rightly deserved the Reformers' accusation of legalism.

The Reformers, on the other hand, were correct in their solution; the Bible clearly teaches that believing sinners are justified on the basis of the life and death of Jesus substituting for their own sinful life (see Romans 10:4; Acts 13:39). The Reformers, nevertheless, were ethically wrong in their definition of substitution—that the doing and dying of Christ was accepted *instead* of our doing and dying. As the Catholic theologians pointed out, it is a fundamental principle of all law, God's or man's, that guilt or punishment cannot be transferred from the guilty to the innocent, nor can the righteousness of one person be legally transferred to another (see Deuteronomy 24:16; 2 Kings 14:6; Ezekiel 18:1-20).

What, then, are we to make of the biblical teaching of substitution? How are we to define it? Biblically, the doctrine of substitution is based on the concept of solidarity or corporate oneness. As we saw earlier, all humanity stands legally condemned because all sinned in one man, Adam. Likewise, God can legally justify sinners because all humanity corporately obeyed the law in one Man, Jesus Christ—the second Adam. God made this possible by uniting His Son with the corporate life of the human race at the incarnation. This qualified Christ to be the second Adam and to be the legal Substitute for fallen humanity.

The Reformers failed to solve the ethical problem of the gospel for the simple reason that they, like the Roman Catholic Church, made a distinction between the humanity of Christ and the humanity He came to redeem. Only when we identify the humanity of Christ with the corporate fallen humanity that He came to redeem can we preach an ethical gospel that is unconditional good news. In other words, humanity that Christ did not assume, He could not save.

The humanity of Christ

In the next chapter, we will study how the Bible clearly defines the concept of substitution through the idea of the "two Adams."

But first, we need to answer two vital questions concerning the humanity of Christ. The first question is: "What was the primary purpose of Christ becoming a man?" Today, there are three answers to this question being given within the Christian church.

1. *Christ became a man to prove that men and women can keep God's law.* The problem with this answer is that we cannot explicitly substantiate it from Scripture. Of course, the fact that in His humanity Christ did perfectly keep the law proves that human beings who are controlled by God's Spirit also can fully meet the law's demands. But the Bible does not teach that this was the primary reason Christ became a man.

2. *Christ became a man to be our example.* The Bible does point to Christ as our example, but it does so only with reference to those who have accepted Him by faith and who have experienced the new birth (see 1 Peter 2:21; Philippians 2:5-8). It does not teach that the primary reason Christ became a man was to be our Example. Those who emphasize Christ as our Example without first clearly presenting Him as our Saviour give the impression that they are teaching the example theory of the atonement. This is why they are often accused of the heresy of perfectionism or legalism.

3. *Christ became a man to redeem men and women from sin.* Scripture presents this as the primary reason for the Son of God being made flesh (see Matthew 1:21; Galatians 4:4, 5; Hebrews 2:14-17). At the very heart of the doctrine of Christology is the glorious truth that Christ assumed humanity so that He could be the Saviour of the world. Only to those who have first received Him as Saviour does He become an Example.

Once we establish that the primary reason Christ became a man was to redeem fallen humanity, we face the second important question concerning His human nature. "*How* did Christ save mankind in His humanity?" Again, Christianity offers more than one answer. Each answer demands a different view of the nature of Christ's humanity.

1. *Christ, in His humanity, saved men and women vicariously (one person acting in the place of another).* The Reformers held this view, as do many evangelical Christians today. To do so, they teach that Christ took on a pre-Fall human nature—the spiritual nature Adam had before he sinned. Here is their basic line of reasoning.

Sin, say those who hold this view, is a dual problem. It is first of all a condition or state of being. A sinful nature is itself sin and automatically stands condemned. Therefore, Christ had to take a sinless human nature (like Adam's before the Fall) in order to substitute Himself vicariously for our sinful nature, which stands condemned. They insist that if Christ had taken our sinful nature as we know it, He would automatically have become a sinner and in need of a savior Himself.

Second, they say, sin is also performance—sinful acts. Christ's perfect life and sacrificial death substitute for our sinful performance. Therefore, those who hold this view see Christ dealing with this dual aspect of sin. His sinless human nature vicariously substituted for our sinful natures. And His perfect performance—His doing and dying—vicariously redeemed us from sin.

However, this position presents two problems.

It makes the gospel unethical. As we have already seen, no law of God or man will allow guilt or righteousness to be transferred from one person to another. So those who teach vicarious substitution are rightly accused of teaching "legal fiction" or a "passed-on righteousness." Attempts to solve this ethical problem (such as "Christ is above the law," or "He volunteered to die in our stead, so this makes it ethical") are unacceptable. Law simply will not allow sin to be transferred from the guilty to the innocent. Only when the guilty and the innocent are actually linked together, as illustrated in the Old Testament sanctuary service, does substitution become legally acceptable (see 1 Corinthians 10:18).

The second problem with the idea of a salvation based on vicarious substitution is that it very easily turns the gospel into "cheap grace." If Christ did it all without having to identify Himself with us, if He lived and died *instead of* us, then we should be able to receive the blessings of His holy life and death simply by agreeing mentally to this truth. We don't have to identify ourselves with His living and dying—as true faith and baptism demand us to do (see Galatians 2:19, 20; Romans 6:1-4). We simply accept that Christ lived and died *instead* of us. That is "cheap grace."

There is a second answer to the question of how Christ saved us in His humanity.

2. *Christ, in His humanity, saved men and women in actuality*—

not vicariously. Those who take this position teach that Christ took the human nature Adam had after his fall. They argue that since Christ came to save fallen humanity, He had to assume the sinful human nature that needed redeeming. By thus identifying Himself with our corporate fallen humanity, Christ qualified Himself to be the second Adam and legally gained the right to be our Substitute.

According to this view, Christ's life and death actually changed mankind's past. Because each of us was corporately identified with Christ's humanity, His life and death became our life and death. In Him, we lived a perfect life; in Him we died the penalty for sin. When Christ died on the cross, all humanity was legally justified because all humanity died with Him there. Justification by faith is simply making that legal justification effective in the life of the believer. Faith, therefore, becomes much more than a mere mental assent to the truth. It requires a heart appreciation of the cross; it produces a surrender of the will and an obedience to the truth as it is in Christ (see Romans 1:5; 6:17; 10:16; Galatians 5:7; 2 Thessalonians 1:7, 8). Such obedience of faith is the basis of true holy living (see Galatians 2:20; Romans 6:10-13).

But some raise a serious question about this view. "If Christ identified Himself with our sinful human nature," they ask, "does that not make Him a sinner like us and in need of a savior as we are?" A sinful nature, they remind us, is itself sin.

It's true that Paul clearly teaches that the sinful human nature we possess is indwelt by sin (see Romans 7:20, 23) and that we are, therefore, "by nature children of wrath" (Ephesians 2:3). It's also true, however, that the Bible clearly teaches that Christ took the same nature as that of the human race He came to redeem (see Hebrews 2:14-17). How, then, are we to resolve the dilemma?

The correct solution is to take note of the qualifying word the New Testament writers use when they speak of the humanity Christ assumed. In John 1:14; Galatians 4:4; and 2 Corinthians 5:21, for example, the writers stop short of saying that in His humanity Christ was just as we are in our fallen humanity. They say He "was *made* flesh" (John 1:14); that He was *"made* of a woman" (Galatians 4:4). What does this word mean?

The Greek words translated *made* in our English Bibles mean *to become.* When Christ became a man, He actually *became what He was not.* The sinful nature He assumed was not His by native right, but something He *took* upon Himself, or *was made to be* in order to redeem it. As Ellen White says, "He took upon His sinless [divine] nature our sinful [human] nature, that He might know how to succor those that are tempted" (*Medical Ministry*, p. 181). The words *"took part"* (Hebrews 2:14) and the word *"likeness"* (Romans 8:3) carry the same connotation as the word *"made."*

Scripture teaches that Christ actually did *assume* our condemned sinful human nature as we know it. But He totally defeated "the law of sin and death" (Romans 8:2) that resided in that sinful human nature and then executed it on the cross. Had Christ consented, even by a thought, to the sinful desires of that nature which He assumed, then He would have become a sinner in need of a savior Himself. That is why, in dealing with the human nature of Christ, we must be exceedingly careful not to drag His mind or His choice into sin or to say that He "had" a sinful nature.

The fact that the New Testament writers record the genealogy of Jesus, tracing His roots to David (see Romans 1:3), to Abraham (see Matthew 1:1-16), and even to Adam (see Luke 3:23-38) clearly shows that Christ's humanity was part and parcel of the humanity He came to redeem. The question that confronts us is: "How and when did Christ cleanse that humanity from the law of sin and death?" Most Christians teach that this took place at the incarnation. But Scripture does not support this. On the contrary, the Bible teaches clearly that it was on the cross that Jesus took away the sin of the world (see Romans 8:2, 3). The incarnation is not God's solution to our sin problem; His solution is "the blood of Jesus Christ his Son [that] cleanseth us from all sin" (1 John 1:7). The incarnation qualified Jesus to be our Substitute and Saviour, but it is the cross that is the power of God unto salvation.

When the everlasting gospel is understood in the light of the "in Christ" motif, the humanity of Jesus becomes everything to us. Today, more and more scholars are recognizing this truth. Here are what two have to say on the subject:

Perhaps the most fundamental truth which we have to learn in the Christian church, or rather relearn since we have suppressed it, is that the Incarnation was the coming of God to save us in the heart of our fallen and depraved humanity, where humanity is at its wickedest in its enmity and violence against the reconciling love of God. That is to say, the Incarnation is to be understood as the coming of God to take upon Himself our fallen human nature, our actual human existence laden with sin and guilt, our humanity diseased in mind and soul in its estrangement or alienation from the Creator. This is a doctrine found everywhere in the early church in the first five centuries, expressed again and again in terms that the whole man had to be assumed by Christ if the whole man was to be saved, that the unassumed is unhealed, or that what God has not taken up in Christ is not saved.... Thus the Incarnation had to be understood as the sending of the Son of God in the concrete form of our own sinful nature and as a sacrifice for sin in which He judged sin within that very nature in order to redeem man from his carnal, hostile mind (Thomas F. Torrance, *The Mediation of Christ*, pp. 48, 49).

It was to be right in sin's own realm that the Son was to bring sin to judgment, overcome it, and take away its power. It is therefore important that with Christ it is actually a matter of "sinful flesh," of *sinful flesh*. . . . Christ's carnal nature was no unreality, but simple, tangible fact. He shared all our conditions. He was under that same power of destruction. Out of "the flesh" arose for Him the same temptations as for us. But in all this He was master of sin (Anders Nygren, *Commentary on Romans*, pp. 314, 315).

The God-man Saviour

At the incarnation, two distinct natures were united in one Person—Jesus Christ. In order for Christ to qualify legally to be our substitute and representative, His divinity had to be united to our corporate fallen humanity that needed redeeming. These two distinct, opposite natures were united in one Person, and Christ became the second Adam. This is the "in Christ" motif, the central theme of Paul's theology. In chart form, here is what the New Testament says about the divinity and humanity that were united in Christ:

His divine nature— What He is:	His human nature— What He was made:
1. Son of God (Luke 1:35).	1. Son of man (Luke 19:10).

2. Self-existing
   (John 1:4).
	2. Born of a woman
	   (Galatians 4:4).

3. Spirit (John 4:24).	3. Flesh (John 1:14).

4. Equal with God
   (Philippians 2:6).
	4. A slave of God
	   (Philippians 2:7).

5. Sinless (2 Corinthians 5:21).	5. Sin (2 Corinthians 5:21).
6. Independent (John 10:18).	6. Dependent (John 5:19, 30).
7. Immortal (1 Timothy 1:17).	7. Mortal (Hebrews 2:14, 15).
8. Lawgiver (James 4:12).	8. Under law (Galatians 4:4).

At the resurrection, these two natures became one, sharing the same divine life. On the cross our corporate, condemned life died eternally in Christ (see 2 Corinthians 5:14). In the resurrection, God gave the human race the eternal life of His Son (see 1 John 5:11). All that we are as a result of the Fall, Christ was made at the incarnation so that through His life, death, and resurrection we could be made, in Him, all that He is (see 2 Corinthians 5:17). This is the good news of the gospel.

By nature we are:

1. spiritually dead, but in Christ were made spiritually alive (see Ephesians 2:5).

2. sinners, but in Christ were made righteous (see 2 Corinthians 5:21).

3. sinful, but in Christ were made holy and blameless (see Ephesians 1:4).

4. condemned, but in Christ were justified (see Romans 5:18).

5. sons of man, but in Christ were made sons of God (see 1 John 3:1).

6. hell bound, but in Christ were made to sit in heavenly places (see Ephesians 2:6).

7. mortal, but in Christ were made immortal (see 2 Timothy 1:8-10).

8. poor, but in Christ were made rich (see 2 Corinthians 8:9).

9. lower than the angels, but in Christ were made joint heirs with Christ (see Hebrews 2:6-12; Romans 8:17).

The next chapter will examine in more detail what Scripture has to say about the two Adams and the implications for you and me.

Key Points in Chapter 4
Christ Our Substitute

1. Justification by faith raises an ethical issue: How can God justify believing sinners and at the same time maintain His integrity to the divine law that justly condemns them to eternal death? (See Romans 4:5; Galatians 3:10.)

2. During the Reformation, the Reformers answered this question with the doctrine of substitution in which Christ's righteousness substitutes for the believer's lack of righteousness.

3. Catholic scholars argued that substitution was unethical. It made God testify to a lie—declaring a sinner justified who is still a sinner. They insisted that before God could *declare* a person justified, He had to *make* the person righteous through an infused grace.

3. The Catholic scholars were ethically right—God does need to make sinners righteous before He can legally declare them to be righteous. They were wrong in their solution to the problem, however.

4. The Reformers were right in their solution to the problem—the Bible clearly teaches that sinners are justified on the basis of the life and death of Jesus substituting for their own sinful life (see Romans 10:4; Acts 13:39). The Reformers were ethically wrong, however, in defining substitution as Jesus' life and death being accepted *instead of* our life and death.

5. Biblically, the doctrine of substitution is based on the concept of corporate oneness. God can legally justify sinners because all humanity corporately obeyed the law in one Man, Jesus Christ. Only when we identify the humanity of Jesus with the corporate fallen humanity He came to redeem can we teach an ethical gospel that is unconditional good news.

6. The main reason Christ became a man was to redeem men and women from sin—not primarily to prove that they could keep God's law or to be their Example (see Matthew 1:21; Galatians 4:4, 5; Hebrews 2:14-17).

7. Christ, in His humanity, saved men and women in actuality—not vicariously. Christ's life and death actually changed humanity's past; Christ's life and death became our life and death. In Him we lived a perfect life; in Him we died the

penalty for sin (see 2 Corinthians 5:14).

8. The Bible clearly teaches that Christ took the same nature as that of the human race He came to redeem (see Hebrews 2:14-17). But it stops short of saying that in His humanity Christ was just as we are in our fallen humanity. The Bible says He "was *made* flesh" (John 1:14). He became something He was not. He took sinful nature upon Himself in order to redeem it.

Chapter Five

The Two Adams: Romans 5

The teaching of the two Adams is one of the most neglected and misunderstood doctrines of the Bible. Yet it is vitally important to our salvation because the eternal destiny of all who have ever lived is closely connected with these two men—Adam and Christ, who is the "second Adam."

As we saw in the previous chapter, God created all mankind in one man—Adam (see Genesis 1:27, 28; Acts 17:26). Likewise, Satan ruined all mankind in one man—Adam (see Romans 5:12, 18; 1 Corinthians 15:21, 22). And God redeemed all mankind in one Man—Christ Jesus, the second Adam (see 1 Corinthians 1:30; Ephesians 1:3; 2:5, 6). Scripture is clear that "in Adam all die" and that "in Christ shall all be made alive" (1 Corinthians 15:22).

It is my conviction that we can never fully understand all the implications and privileges of our salvation "in Christ" until we come to realize our situation "in Adam." Two New Testament passages—Romans 5:12-21 and 1 Corinthians 15:19-23; 45-49—explain in detail this important teaching of the two Adams. Let's look carefully at what they have to say.

Romans 5:12-21

In Romans 5:11, the apostle Paul states a glorious truth of the gospel. He says that we Christians can rejoice because *we have already received the atonement.* Paul then goes on to explain in verses 12-21 *how* we have received this atonement. He does so by using Adam as a type, or pattern, of Christ (see verse 14). He argues that we are redeemed "in Christ" in the same way that we are lost "in Adam." The history of these two men—Adam and Christ—has affected the eternal destiny of all mankind. In order to use Adam as a pattern of Christ, Paul first explains, in verses 12-14, what our situation is "in Adam."

"By one man sin entered into the world, and death by sin; and so death passed upon all men, for that all have sinned" (Romans 5:12). In this verse, Paul makes three statements about the sin problem. He says that sin entered the world (that is, human history) through one man—Adam. Second, he says that this sin condemned Adam to death. Third, Paul says that this death spread to all humanity "for that all have sinned." This last phrase has generated endless controversies in the history of the Christian church. Did Paul mean that all die because "all have sinned" *personally as did Adam*? Or did he mean that all die because "all have sinned" *in Adam*?

The conclusion we reach has important implications for our salvation, since Paul's purpose in discussing Adam is to use him as a pattern of Christ. I believe that when we carefully consider the context of this passage and the logic of Paul's argument, as well as his teaching regarding justification by faith elsewhere throughout the New Testament, we must conclude that Paul is saying here in Romans 5:12 that death spread to all mankind because "all have sinned" *in Adam*. Paul's logic is that all humanity was "in Adam" when he sinned, and therefore the whole human race was implicated, or participated, in Adam's act of disobedience. Hence, Paul says, the condemnation of death that came to Adam automatically passed on to every human being. I see five reasons to believe that this is what Paul is saying in this verse.

1. It simply isn't true that everyone dies because they have personally sinned as Adam did. Babies, for example, die even though they have no personal sins. The only explanation for the fact that death is universal is that all sinned "in Adam."

2. Grammatically, the Greek verb *sinned* in verse 12 is in the *aorist* tense. This tense normally refers to an act that took place in the past at a single point in time. Grammatically, then, "all have sinned" most naturally refers to a single past historical event (Adam's sin) and not to the continuing personal sins of his

descendants over the centuries.

3. Paul goes on to explain in verses 13 and 14 what he meant in verse 12. He says that all those who lived from Adam until Moses died even though they "had not sinned after the similitude [likeness] of Adam's transgression" (verse 14). Therefore, the immediate context of verse 12 contradicts the idea that all die because they have sinned as Adam sinned.

4. Four times in Romans 5:15-18 Paul explicitly states that Adam's sin (not our own personal sins) brought judgment, condemnation, and death to the whole human race. Thus the context of verse 12 clearly supports the idea that all die because "all have sinned" in Adam. In verse 19 Paul sums up his argument in unmistakable language. He says, "By one man's disobedience many were made sinners."

5. The logic of Paul's argument in this passage is that Adam is a type, or pattern, of Christ—that what happened to us in Adam is undone for us in Christ. Therefore, if we insist that verse 12 means that all men die because "all have sinned" as Adam sinned—then we must make the analogy fit by arguing that all men live (or are justified) because all have obeyed as Christ obeyed. Such an argument turns justification by faith into salvation by works, the very opposite of Paul's clear teaching in Romans. Paul's analogy here is that since "all have sinned" in Adam and are therefore condemned to death in him, so all have obeyed in Christ and therefore stand justified to life in Him (see verse 18).

Now verses 13 and 14 make sense. In these verses, Paul is simply proving what he stated in verse 12—that all die because "all have sinned" in Adam. He does this by looking at a segment of the human race, those who lived from Adam until Moses. To be sure these people were sinning, but since God had not yet explicitly spelled out His law until He gave to it to mankind as a legal code through Moses, He could not justly condemn these people to death for their personal sins. This is what Paul is saying in verse 13. Nevertheless, they *were* dying, as Paul points out in verse 14. Why? His answer is that they were dying because all humanity stands condemned to death *in Adam*.

In spite of what seems to me to be the clear evidence of Romans 5, some still feel they can harmonize Paul's logic in these verses with the idea that all men and women die because all have sinned personally as did Adam. They do so by insisting that the death Paul says we receive "in Adam" is only the first, or "sleep" death. We receive the "second" death—eternal death—they say, as a result of our own personal sins. Such reasoning will not stand the test of Scripture, no matter how convincing it may sound. Paul uses the word *death* twice in Romans 5:12—once to refer to Adam and next to refer to humanity, Adam's posterity. In other words, Paul says the same death that came to Adam passed on to all humanity. What death was that—the first death or the second?

Before the Fall, Adam surely knew nothing about the first death. Therefore, the death sentence pronounced on Adam when he sinned was the second death—eternal death. It was goodbye to life forever. Had there been no "lamb slain from the foundation of the world" (Revelation 13:8), Adam would have forfeited his life forever the day he sinned, and mankind would have died eternally in him (see Genesis 2:17). It is this death—the second death—that has passed to all mankind "in Adam." In Adam the whole human race belongs legally on death row. It is only in Christ that we can pass from eternal death to eternal life (see John 5:24; 1 Corinthians 15:55-57; 2 Timothy 1:10; Revelation 20:6).

We must be very careful at this point not to go beyond what Scripture says. We must *not* teach that in Adam all humanity also inherits his guilt. This is the heresy of "original sin" introduced by Augustine and adopted by the Roman Catholic Church. Guilt, in a legal sense, always includes personal volition or responsibility, and God does not hold us personally responsible for something in which we had no choice. Only when we personally, consciously, deliberately, persistently, and ultimately reject the gift of eternal life in Christ does the guilt and responsibility of sin and the second death become ours (see John 3:18, 36; Mark 16:15; Hebrews 2:1-4; 10:14, 26-29).

Once Paul has established our situation in Adam (see Romans 5:12-14), he goes on to show how Adam is a type, or pattern, of Christ (see verses 15-18). He argues that just as Adam's sin affected all humanity for death, likewise, what Christ did as the second Adam also affected all humanity for life. When Adam sinned, Paul says, he brought the judgment of condemnation and death to "all men." In the same way, when Christ obeyed, He not only redeemed humanity from the results of Adam's sin, but much more He canceled all our personal sins ("many offenses") and brought the verdict of "justification of life" to all men (verses 16, 18). This is the unconditional good news that the gospel proclaims.

In verse 19, Paul adds another dimension to the problem Adam's sin caused for us. It "made" all men into sinners. This means that in addition to condemnation and the death sentence that we received "in Adam," we are also born slaves to sin and are therefore incapable, in and of ourselves, of producing genuine righteousness (see Romans 3:9-12; 7:14-25). But in the second half of verse 19, Paul reminds us that because of Christ's obedience we shall "be made righteous." Notice Paul uses the future tense here—"shall be made righteous"—indicating that this applies to those who receive Jesus Christ (see verse 17). To demonstrate that Adam's sin has made us slaves to sin, God gave His law (see verse 20; Romans 7:7-13). In other words, Paul is clear that God did not give us His law to *solve* the sin problem but to *expose* it. The law showed how Adam's one sin ("the offence," verse 20) has produced a whole race of sinners. Again, the good news is that although sin multiplied through Adam's fall, God's grace in Christ has multiplied all the more (see verse 20).

This brings us to the next important point concerning Romans 5. Notice that in this chapter, Paul mentions two things in connection with our situation in Christ that he does *not* apply to our situation in Adam. First, Paul refers to what God accomplished "in Christ" for all humanity as a "free gift" (verse 16). This means that although all have been legally justified in Christ's doing and dying, justification is still a gift. Like any gift, it belongs only to those who accept it. Only those who by faith receive God's gift of justification will enjoy the benefits of Christ's obedience. Paul makes this clear in verse 17.

Second, Paul repeatedly uses the expression "much more" when pointing to the blessings we receive through Christ's obedience. In Christ, much more has been accomplished than simply undoing the damage we inherit from Adam. For example, by His death Christ not only liberated humanity from the condemnation of death resulting from Adam's one sin. Much more, He redeemed us from our own "many [personal] offenses unto justification" (verse 16). In Christ, not only do we receive eternal life, but much more we shall "reign in life by one, Jesus Christ" (verse 17). This is superabundant grace.

Thus Paul concludes "where sin abounded, grace did much more abound" (verse 20). As sin rules our lives from birth and results in death, Paul pleads for us to let grace now take over and reign in our lives, producing righteousness, until eternity is ushered in (see verse 21).

What conclusions, then, can we draw concerning our salvation from Paul's argument of the two Adams in Romans 5?

1. Whether I am reckoned a sinner and condemned to death, or whether I am declared righteous and qualify for eternal life, has to do with the history of Adam or of Christ. On the basis of Adam's disobedience I am reckoned a sinner; on the basis of Christ's obedience I am declared justified or righteous.

2. If I belong to the humanity produced by Adam, I am made a sinner and am condemned to eternal death. If, however, I belong to the humanity initiated by Christ, I am declared righteous and qualify for eternal life. In other words, my eternal destiny rests upon which humanity I choose to belong to.

3. All of us by creation are "in Adam." This is the hopeless situation we inherit by birth into the human race. Hence we are "by nature the children of wrath" (Ephesians 2:3). But the good news is that God has given us a new identity and history "in Christ." This is His supreme gift to humanity. Our position "in Adam" is by birth. Our position "in Christ" is by faith. What God has done for the whole human race in Christ is given as a "free gift," something we do not deserve. That is why the gift is referred to as grace or unmerited favor. To be experienced, this gift must be received, and it is made effective by faith alone.

4. Adam and Christ belong to opposite camps that cannot be reconciled. Adam is equated with sin and death; Christ with righteousness and life. Consequently, it is impossible for anyone to belong, subjectively, to Adam and Christ at the same time. To accept Christ by faith means to renounce totally our position in Adam (see 2 Corinthians 5:17; 6:14-16). Baptism is a public declaration that we have died to sin (our position in Adam) and have been resurrected into newness of life (our position in Christ). See Romans 6:1-4, 8; 2 Timothy 2:11.

5. Thus, the human race can be divided into two groups: (1) the

Adamic race, made up of many nations and tribes (see Acts 17:26), and (2) believers who are all one in Christ (see Romans 12:5; 1 Corinthians 10:17; Galatians 3:27, 28; Ephesians 4:11-13). Because of the gospel, we have the choice to belong to either of these two groups. We may retain our position in Adam by unbelief—and reap the results of his sin. Or, by faith, we may become united to Christ and receive the benefits of His righteousness.

This is Paul's teaching in Romans 5 regarding the two Adams. In the next chapter we will examine what he has to say on this subject in 1 Corinthians 15 and then draw some conclusions for our own experience.

Key Points in Chapter 5
The Two Adams: Romans 5

1. In Romans 5, Paul says that men and women *have already received* the atonement. He supports this statement by using Adam as a pattern of Christ, whom he calls the "second Adam." Paul's argument is that we are redeemed "in Christ" the same way we are lost "in Adam."

2. For Paul, "in Adam" means that all humanity stands condemned to death because we were all corporately "in Adam" when he sinned.

3. Likewise, for Paul "in Christ" means that all humanity has been justified because we were all corporately "in Christ" when He obeyed and died.

4. Paul does *not* mean that all humanity inherits Adam's guilt. This is the heresy of "original sin."

5. In Romans 5, Paul mentions two things in connection with our situation "in Christ" that he does not apply to our situation "in Adam":

   a. What God accomplished for us "in Christ" is a free gift. Although we all have been justified corporately in Christ's life and death, justification is still a gift that belongs only to those who accept it.

   b. In Christ, much more has been accomplished than simply undoing the condemnation we inherit from Adam. God's grace will abound in our lives to reign and produce righteousness.

6. Paul's argument in Romans 5 concerning the two Adams can be summed up as follows: On the basis of Adam's disobedience, we are reckoned as sinners; on the basis of Christ's obedience we are declared justified.

Chapter Six

The Two Adams: 1 Corinthians 15

In 1 Corinthians 15, Paul repeats to the Christians in Corinth the same ideas regarding the two Adams he had presented to the Roman believers in Romans 5. Briefly, here is what Paul is saying in 1 Corinthians 15:19-23; 45-49.

Verses 19, 20. Correcting those who denied the resurrection, Paul points out that the great hope of the Christian is to be raised to life. Christ Himself rose from the dead and is the "firstfruits" of those who are resting in their graves "in Christ." Paul goes on to explain that this hope is not built on the foundation of our goodness, but on our position "in Christ."

Verse 21. Since death came to the whole human race through one man (notice that the word *man* is singular and refers to Adam according to the next verse), so through one Man (Christ) came resurrection from death.

Verse 22. Death came upon all of us because of our position "in Adam." Likewise, resurrection and the hope of eternal life come to everyone who is "in Christ." The expressions "in Adam" and "in Christ" imply solidarity or corporate oneness.

Verse 23. Christ, the prototype of all who are in Him, has already risen from the dead, thus guaranteeing that those who are His will be resurrected at His coming.

Verse 45. The first Adam was a created being—that is, his life had a beginning and can therefore have an end. The second Adam

(Christ) introduced the life-giving spirit, or eternal life.

Verse 47. The first man, Adam, was made from the dust of the earth; his character was likewise carnal, earthly. The second man, Christ, was from heaven. His character was spiritual, godly.

Verse 48. Just as the children of the earthly Adam reflect his earthly (sinful) nature and character, so those who belong to the heavenly Christ will reflect His heavenly (righteous) nature and character.

Verse 49. Just as we all, by nature, are a reproduction of the earthly image of Adam, so likewise we shall reflect fully the image of Christ's resurrected nature at the second coming (see 1 Corinthians 15:50-54; Romans 8:23-25; Philippians 3:20, 21).

According to 1 Corinthians 15:21-23, 45-49, there have been only two heads of the human race—Adam and Christ, who is the "last Adam" (verse 45). The destiny of the entire human race rests upon these two. Adam is the prototype of unredeemed humanity; Christ is the prototype of redeemed humanity. What is true of Adam is true of those who are "in him," and what is true of Christ is true of those who are "in Him." Adam's situation after the Fall is the situation of all the unredeemed. That which Christ realized for all mankind will be the situation of the redeemed. "As in Adam all die, even so in Christ shall all be made alive" (1 Corinthians 15:22).

Christ's resurrection is the guarantee that all who belong to Him by faith will be raised to life at the second coming. Christ's righteousness, not our self-righteousness, qualifies us for heaven—now and in the judgment.

In verse 45, Paul calls Christ the "last Adam." In verse 47, he refers to Him as the "second man." These terms have important implications. As the "last Adam," Christ was the sum total of all that is comprehended in the "first Adam." As the "second man," He is the head of a new, redeemed race. Having gathered unto Himself all those who belonged to the first Adam, Christ superseded the whole Adamic race when He died on the cross. There He met the just demands of the law on our behalf (see 2 Corinthians 5:14; 1 Peter 2:24) and died the second death as the representative of the whole human race (see Hebrews 2:9). In this way He abolished death (see 2 Timothy 1:10).

Then, by His resurrection, Christ qualified to be the "second man," the head of a new redeemed humanity who are "in Him" (see 2 Corinthians 5:17).

The two Adams summarized

Let's summarize what we have learned from this detailed study of Paul's teaching about the two Adams.

1. Adam's sin brought all humanity under the death sentence—both the first and second deaths. The first death became necessary because the gospel shielded us from immediately suffering the actual wages of sin, the second death.

2. Christ's obedience saved all humanity from the second death and pronounced the verdict of justification on all mankind. On the cross Christ experienced and abolished only the second death, the curse of the law (see Hebrews 2:9; 2 Timothy 1:10; Galatians 3:13). Since believers die the first death, the gospel obviously redeems us only from the second death (see Revelation 20:6).

3. The whole force of the parallel between Adam and Christ (see Romans 5:12-21) depends on the idea of the solidarity of mankind in Adam and in Christ. Of the 510 times the word *Adam* appears in the Old Testament, the great majority possess a collective significance. In the same sense, the New Testament calls Christ the "last" or "second" Adam.

4. Salvation from the second death and the verdict of justification to life is God's supreme gift in Christ to all humanity (see John 3:16). This is the good news of the gospel. But like any gift, it has to be received in order to be enjoyed (see Romans 5:17). Those who knowingly, willfully, persistently reject God's gift of salvation in Christ are deliberately choosing the second death. Therefore, in the judgment God bestows on them what they have deliberately and persistently chosen. They can blame only themselves (and they will) when they face the second death (see John 3:18, 36; Mark 16:15, 16; Romans 14:11).

5. Every baby is born subjectively under the reign of sin, condemnation, and death because of Adam's fall (see Romans 3:9-20). If we continue to live under this reign of sin and resist the grace of Christ, we will experience the second death. But objectively, Christ has delivered each of us from this reign of sin by His doing and dying; He has placed us under the reign of grace, righteousness, and eternal life. To accept this gift by faith is to say

goodbye to sin and death and to say hello to eternal life (see Romans 5:21; 6:14, 22, 23).

6. We cannot choose to remain in Adam and at the same time accept by faith to be in Christ. To receive Christ, the author of righteousness, means to renounce Adam, the author of sin (see Romans 6:15-18).

7. Our eternal destiny depends on which humanity we have chosen. Unbelief means deliberately choosing to remain "in Adam" and the reign of sin and death. Belief means deliberately choosing to be "in Christ" and the reign of righteousness and eternal life. This is why God will not bring the sad history of this wicked world to a close until the gospel has been preached "in all the world for a witness" (Matthew 24:14).

God will judge each of us on judgment day based on the deliberate choice we make concerning the two Adams. "I call heaven and earth to record this day against you, that I have set before you life and death, blessing and cursing: therefore choose life, that both thou and thy seed may live" (Deuteronomy 30:19).

Conclusion

The clear teaching of the two Adams is that our hope rests entirely on Christ, our righteousness, for "by the deeds of the law there shall no flesh be justified in his [God's] sight" (Romans 3:20; cf. Galatians 2:16). Those who are justified by faith in Christ shall live (see Romans 1:17; Hebrews 2:4; Philippians 3:9).

At creation, God made Adam from the dust of the earth and breathed into him the breath of life so that Adam became a living person (see Genesis 2:7). The corporate life that Adam received from God was perfect and sinless, dominated by selfless love (*agape*), for he was created in God's image, and God is *agape* (see Genesis 1:26; John 4:24; 1 John 4:8, 16). After God created Adam and his companion, Eve, He commanded them to multiply His life and fill the earth with men and women who would reflect His character (see Genesis 1:28). This was God's original purpose for the world.

Unfortunately, before they could begin the multiplication process, Adam and Eve fell into sin. This affected the corporate life of Adam in three ways:

1. His sinless life became guilty of sin (see Genesis 2:17; 3:6, 7).

2. His guilty life came under the condemnation of the law, the penalty of which is death (see Ezekiel 18:4, 20).

3. His perfect, sinless life became a sinful life. Instead of being under the control of the Spirit of *agape*, it came under the bondage of Satan and sin's self-love (see Isaiah 53:6; John 8:34; Philippians 2:21; 2 Peter 2:19).

Since the whole human race is simply Adam's life multiplied, these three results of Adam's sin passed on to all of us. Thus the life we receive at birth is:

1. a life that has sinned (see Romans 5:12);

2. a life that is condemned by the law. This means that the just demands of the law leave us facing nothing but eternal death (see John 3:36; 1 Corinthians 15:22; Revelation 20:14, 15);

3. a life that is in bondage to sin and the devil (see John 8:34; Romans 7:14; 1 John 3:8).

This is our situation "in Adam," and we can do nothing ourselves to change it. "In Adam" we have all sinned; we are in bondage to sin; we must all die. Without the gospel, in other words, we are hopelessly lost and doomed forever.

Christ was made flesh to deliver us from this situation and to restore God's original purpose for us. He came as the second head of Adam's race and introduced the reign of grace through His perfect life, death, and resurrection. The fallen human race is Adam's sinful life multiplied, but the body of Christ, His church (see Romans 12:5; 1 Corinthians 12:13, 14), is Christ's righteous life multiplied (see Romans 8:29; Hebrews 2:11; 1 John 3:1, 2).

Through His "unspeakable gift" (2 Corinthians 9:15), God has changed our hopeless situation in Adam and has given us a new identity and hope in Christ. At conversion, or the new-birth experience, we receive the very life of Christ (see John 3:3-6). This life, the corporate humanity that Christ assumed and that we receive by faith in Him, is:

1. a life that has perfectly obeyed the law in every detail (see Matthew 5:17; Romans 10:4);

2. a life that has condemned and conquered the power of sin in the flesh (see John 8:46; Romans 8:2, 3);

3. a life that Christ submitted to the full wages of sin on the cross (see Romans 5:8, 10; Philippians 2:8);

4. a life that has overcome death and the grave (1 Corinthians

15:55-58; Hebrews 2:14, 15).

All these facts become reality for us when we receive this life by faith. This life justifies us because it perfectly obeyed the law and met its just demands on behalf of our sins. It is also able to deliver us fully from the slavery of sin and produce in us the very righteousness of God, since it has already accomplished this in Christ's humanity (see 1 Timothy 3:16). Finally, this life will raise us from the dead and guarantee us eternity, for it is eternal life (see John 3:36; 6:27; 1 John 2:25).

All who are "in Christ" have these privileges. As we learn to live by His life, instead of our own natural life, we truly abide in Him (see John 15:4-8). We walk in the light and in the Spirit (see 1 John 1:6, 7; Romans 8:4; Galatians 5:16). In later chapters, we will see that Christ's life abiding in us and dominating us is the means of our sanctification. Paul calls this "Christ in you, the hope of glory" (Colossians 1:27). In Christ, we possess a life that is greater than the power of sin and the devil (see 1 John 4:4). When this new life takes over, sin will be put to death in our lives, and Christ will be revealed (see Romans 8:9-14). This is how the earth will be lightened with the glory of God through His people. This will be God's final display before Christ comes (see Revelation 10:7; 18:1).

The doctrine of the two Adams is of utmost importance to understanding the objective gospel and justification by faith. But it is also of great practical value to our Christian experience because the fruits of this doctrine lead to holy living, or sanctification. "Ye shall know the truth," Jesus said, "and the truth shall make you free" (John 8:32).

Key Points in Chapter 6
The Two Adams: 1 Corinthians 15

1. Adam's sin brought all humanity under the death sentence—both the first and second deaths.
2. Christ's obedience saved all humanity from the second death and pronounced the verdict of justification on all mankind.
3. The force of Paul's parallel between Adam and Christ depends on the idea of the solidarity, or corporate oneness, of mankind in Adam and in Christ (see Romans 5:12-21).
   a. Since the whole human race is simply Adam's life multiplied, the results of his sin have passed on to all of us. The life we receive at birth is a life that (1) has sinned; (2) is condemned to eternal death by the law; and (3) is in bondage to sin and Satan.
   b. Through His "unspeakable gift" (2 Corinthians 9:15), God has given us a new identity in Christ. At conversion, we receive the very life of Christ—the corporate humanity that He assumed. This life has (1) perfectly obeyed the law; (2) condemned and conquered the power of sin; and (3) overcome death and the grave.
4. Salvation from the second death and the verdict of justification to life is God's supreme gift in Christ to all humanity (see John 3:16).
5. Everyone is born subjectively under the reign of sin, condemnation, and death because of Adam's fall (see Romans 3:9-20). But objectively, Christ has delivered each of us by His life and death and has placed us under the reign of grace, righteousness, and eternal life.
6. We cannot choose to remain in Adam and at the same time accept by faith to be in Christ.
7. Our eternal destiny depends on which humanity we choose—that of Adam or that of Christ.

65

Chapter Seven

The Cross and the Great Controversy

The very heart of the New Testament message is the cross. It is the supreme manifestation of God's *agape* love. At the cross, God met the just demands of the law on behalf of the human race; there Jesus Christ demonstrated God's power by defeating Satan and sin. Paul uses "the cross" as a sort of shorthand for the good news, the gospel. He says, "The preaching of the cross is to them that perish foolishness; but unto us which are saved it is the power of God" (1 Corinthians 1:18). No wonder Satan doesn't want us to understand the importance of the cross! No wonder he has shrouded it in darkness, causing the church to lose much of its power!

The devil is quite content for us to decorate our churches with the cross, to print the cross on our books, to hang crosses around our necks, even to preach about the cross—as long as we remain ignorant about the great truth of the cross.

But the truth of the cross will be, must be, restored. Before the end, the light flowing from the cross into the hearts of believers will illuminate the whole earth with God's glory. "Now is the judgment of this world: now shall the prince of this world be cast out," Jesus said. "And I, if I be lifted up from the earth, will draw all men unto me" (John 12:31, 32).

In this chapter and the two chapters following it, we will be looking at the crucial subject of the cross from three viewpoints.

67

The first of these is the cross in the light of the great controversy.

At the cross "that old serpent, called the Devil, and Satan, which deceiveth the whole world" (Revelation 12:9) was totally defeated, judged, and condemned. The great controversy, which began in heaven between Lucifer and Christ, met its determining conclusion at the cross. Here the great deceiver was fully exposed to the whole universe in his true character as a liar and a murderer. Only as we view Satan in the light of the cross will we see him for what he truly is.

In chapter 1, we saw how Lucifer, turned Satan, rebelled against God. He came to the place that he actually wanted to murder God's Son so that he might have Jesus' place of honor (see John 8:44). Following his expulsion from heaven, Satan unlawfully took dominion of this earth from Adam and Eve. He began to use fallen men and women as his tools to develop this world into his own kingdom based on the principle of self-love. For more than four thousand years after Adam's fall, Satan kept secret his inner desire to murder the Son of God.

But one silent night on the hills surrounding Bethlehem, Satan and his angels heard strange music. A group of their old companions were singing, "Glory to God in the highest, and on earth peace, good will toward men" (Luke 2:14). Satan listened as an angel told the shepherds, "Unto you is born this day in the city of David a Saviour, which is Christ the Lord" (verse 11).

Not only was this "good tidings of great joy" (verse 10) to the shepherds; it was good news to Satan as well. Here was a wonderful opportunity to satisfy his long-cherished desire. Now he could carry out what he had wanted to do in heaven—murder the Son of God. What better opportunity would he ever have? Christ, his bitter enemy, had risked His life to come as a helpless baby into the world that Satan controlled. Now he could take his revenge against this hated Foe who had defeated him in heaven and cast him out of his heavenly home!

Satan lost little time. Using Herod the Great as his agent, he schemed to kill Jesus through the decree to destroy every male child under two years old in Bethlehem (see Matthew 2:1-16). But Jesus' hour had not yet come. The Bible is almost silent about Jesus' boyhood and early adult years, yet Satan must have continued trying to accomplish his purpose during this time. Then

Jesus began His ministry, and the Bible records numerous attempts on His life, each one prompted by Satan himself. As just one example, the Bible says "the Jews took up stones *again* to stone him [Jesus]" (John 10:31, emphasis supplied). Repeatedly, Satan prompted men to kill Jesus. All these efforts failed for one reason. "His hour was not yet come" (John 7:30; 8:20).

Then came Gethsemane. Jesus told the Satan-controlled mob that came to arrest Him, "When I was daily with you in the temple, ye stretched forth no hands against me: but this is your hour, and the power of darkness [Satan]" (Luke 22:53). Now Satan was to be allowed to have his way. The hour had come for Satan to be exposed to the universe as a murderer. "He [Satan] was a murderer from the beginning, and abode not in the truth" (John 8:44). Like all sins, murder begins with a cherished desire; it doesn't have to be an act (see Matthew 5:21-28). From the beginning of the great controversy, Satan had murdered Christ in his mind. In heaven, he had wanted to get rid of Him and take His place. Now the time had come.

At the cross, Satan was given full control of Christ to do with Him as he pleased. Satan's hidden desire, cherished in secret so long, could come into the open in no other way. Now the entire universe would be able to see what sin really is and what it will end up doing if it has the opportunity. Sin is rebellion against God and His law of self-sacrificing love. If allowed to have its own way, sin will actually murder God in its hatred of Him.

Jesus told His disciples, "If the world hate you, ye know that it hated me before it hated you" (John 15:18). Why should the world hate Jesus, who went about doing good? Because "the whole world lieth in the wicked one" (1 John 5:19), and the wicked one, Satan, hates Christ. It's not surprising, then, that the Jews followed Satan's urging and screamed, "Away with him, away with him, crucify him" (John 19:15). At the cross, Satan revealed his hatred for God in all its hideous reality. That hatred caused him to put Jesus to public shame, inflict excruciating suffering upon Him, and finally murder Him. Nothing else would satisfy Satan's frenzy.

Besides being a shameful death reserved only for the worst criminals and runaway slaves, crucifixion was also an unusually painful way to die. The flogging that preceded the crucifixion caused great suffering itself—sometimes even death. Then the condemned person was forced to drag his heavy cross on lacerated shoulders to the place of execution. There, nailed alive to the cross, the victim suffered beyond description.

It is of utmost importance that we realize the shame and suffering inflicted on Christ at the cross did *not* come from God. The cross was in God's plan; He allowed it—in part, to expose Satan's true character. But God was not responsible for the cross. It came as a direct result of Satan's hatred and sin. This means that we must never equate the physical suffering and shame Christ endured on the cross with the sacrifice that saves us. We must never confuse what Satan did to Christ on the cross with what God did to His Son there. God and Satan were not partners at the cross.

Satan, who was solely responsible for Christ's physical sufferings on the cross, has somehow deceived Christians into believing that this suffering is the supreme sacrifice that accomplishes our salvation. Never! If so, then Satan has actually contributed to our salvation, and that can never be.

Satan revealed his true nature at the cross. In the eyes of the holy angels and unfallen worlds, this demonstration forever brought about his downfall. But the cross must also unveil Satan's character to us. As Christians, we represent Christ on earth. Therefore, "the offense of the cross" that Christ endured for us must also become ours (see Galatians 5:11). As Christians, we have said goodbye to our position in the world and have been crucified to the world in order to become one with Christ (see John 15:19; 17:16; Galatians 6:14). This means that we have become enemies of Satan and his world. Therefore, what Satan and the world did to Christ on the cross, they will do to us. This is the "offense of the cross" that all true believers must endure.

If the world today does not hate us or put us to shame, it is simply because the world does not see Christ in us. But let Him be revealed in our lives through the power of the gospel, and the world will turn against us immediately. As it did Jesus, the world will hate us (see John 7:7; 17:14; 1 John 3:13), put us to shame (see Acts 5:41), and persecute us to the death (see John 16:33; Romans 8:17, 18; 2 Timothy 3:12).

At the cross, the world under Satan had to make a choice between Christ (in whom Pilate said he could find no fault) and

Barabbas (the worst criminal that could be found in the jail).
Without hesitation, the world chose to release Barabbas and to
crucify Christ. The world today is still under Satan, and it will
make the same choice if forced to choose between one of its own
and the most insignificant, but genuine, believer. This is the cost
of discipleship.

At the time of the cross, the world was divided within itself.
Jews were against Romans; Pharisees against Sadducees. But
Christ was their common enemy, and they united to oppose Him.
Today, the world is also divided into many factions. But let the
character of Christ be reproduced in His church, and the world
will unite against the saints. This will be the great tribulation that
will come at the end of time, when the church will finally demonstrate the power of the gospel.

In heaven, Satan had struggled with Christ and was defeated.
At the cross, they met once more in battle. This time, Satan was
confident of victory, but his victory was turned into defeat once
again—a defeat from which Satan will never recover. Praise the
Lord for such a Saviour!

Key Points in Chapter 7
The Cross and the Great Controversy

1. The great controversy that began in heaven between Lucifer and Christ met its determining conclusion at the cross. Here the deceiver was exposed in his true character to the entire universe.

2. At the cross, Satan was allowed to do with Christ as he pleased. Now the entire universe could see what sin really is and to what lengths it will go.

3. The shame and suffering inflicted on Christ at the cross did *not* come from God; it came as a direct result of Satan's hatred and sin.

4. Satan, who was solely responsible for Christ's physical sufferings on the cross, has somehow deceived Christians into believing that this suffering is the supreme sacrifice that accomplishes our salvation. If so, then Satan has actually contributed to our salvation!

5. The offense of the cross that Jesus endured will also become ours. What Satan and the world did to Christ on the cross, they will attempt to do to us as well.

Chapter Eight

The Cross
and the Atonement

Far more happened at the cross than shame, suffering, and death. On the face of it, Jesus' cruel fate appeared to be a triumph for Satan. But God took this apparent defeat and turned it into a glorious victory by which the whole human race could be saved.

Paul said:

> We preach Christ crucified, unto the Jews a stumblingblock, and unto the Greeks foolishness; but unto them which are called [saved], both Jews and Greeks, Christ the power of God, and the wisdom of God. Because the foolishness of God is wiser than men; and the weakness of God is stronger than men (1 Corinthians 1:23-25).

In this chapter we will look beyond the terrible physical suffering of Christ on the cross to an even more terrible anguish He endured there. His physical suffering, awful as it was, played no part in our atonement. Jesus' physical pain came from Satan and the cruel men he inspired. But the supreme sacrifice, the means by which sinners are reconciled to a holy and righteous God, came from another source.

Not only did the cross fully reveal Satan's malignant hatred, it also revealed the depths of God's *agape* love. "The Word was made flesh and dwelt among us, (and we beheld his glory, the glory as of the only begotten of the Father,) full of grace and truth" (John 1:14).

At the cross of Christ, God's glory, His self-sacrificing love, was fully displayed. Like the disciples, we too must behold that glory if we are to grow into the fullness of His image. "But we all, with open face beholding as in a glass the glory of the Lord, are changed into the same image from glory to glory, even as by the Spirit of the Lord" (2 Corinthians 3:18). Against the cross's dark background of sin and Satan, God manifested His glory in all its brilliance. Let's examine that glory—what it was and what it means to us. As we do so, let's lay aside all preconceived ideas and behold the truth as it is in Christ and Him crucified.

We can appreciate the significance of the cross only as we realize what sin has done to us. Sin separates us from God (see Isaiah 59:2). It makes us enemies of God (see Romans 5:10). Thus we need to be reconciled to God, brought into harmony and oneness with Him. That is what the word *atonement* means— that sinful human beings have been reconciled to God, brought into "oneness" with Him. Scripture is clear that it is Christ who has reconciled us to God and that He accomplished this at the cross (see 2 Corinthians 5:18, 19; Hebrews 2:17; Ephesians 2:16; Romans 5:10). How did He do this? How did the death of Christ reconcile us to God?

Besides being something that God hates and cannot tolerate, sin is "the transgression of the law" (1 John 3:4). He has made it absolutely clear that "the wages of sin is death" (Romans 6:23, cf. Genesis 2:16, 17; Ezekiel 18:4, 20). And this penalty of sin is not just death, but *eternal* death.

Scripture brings to view two kinds of death. There is the first death, which the Bible refers to as a "sleep" (see John 11:11-14; 1 Corinthians 15:51; 1 Thessalonians 4:14). This is the common experience of all humanity—saved and lost alike. Then there is the second death, which is an eternal death. It is goodbye to life forever. This is the death that the lost will experience at the end of the millennium (see Revelation 2:11; 20:6, 14; 21:8). The first death, terrible as it appears to us, is not the wages of sin. It is only the *consequence* of sin. Therefore all who die the first death will be resurrected—the saved to eternal life, and the lost to face the second death, the wages of sin. In the second death, God, the

Source of all life, abandons the unrepentant to their own choice of unbelief, leaving them without any hope whatsoever. Christ's death on the cross was "unto sin" (Romans 6:10). This simply means that as our substitute and representative He experienced on the cross the "second death," the eternal death that the Bible describes as "the wages of sin." As Hebrews 2:9 puts it, He "by the grace of God should taste death for every man."

The Scripture promises that those who have accepted by faith their position in Christ, and who will be raised in the first resurrection, will escape the second death. "Blessed and holy is he that hath part in the first resurrection: on such the second death hath no power" (Revelation 20:6). Why do these avoid the second death? It is because Christ, their Sin Bearer, has already "tasted" the second death for them (see Hebrews 2:9). On the cross, Christ actually experienced the second death on behalf of fallen humanity. It was this that constituted the supreme sacrifice.

By deceiving the church into believing that men and women have immortal souls, Satan has enshrouded in darkness the glorious truth of what really happened on the cross. You see, if we possess an immortal soul, then death simply becomes a separation of the soul from the body. The second death—eternal death—becomes impossible, for the soul continues to live after the body dies. That is why the Christian church as a whole has focused on Christ's physical suffering at the crucifixion as His supreme sacrifice for mankind, although in reality His physical suffering was no different in nature or degree than that suffered by many humans throughout history. This is the reason, too, that most Christians believe the wages of sin to be, not eternal death, but eternal torture in the flames of hell.

By causing the church to view the cross from the Roman perspective, Satan has obscured the real sacrifice of Christ. Only when we look at the cross from the Jewish point of view, as did the New Testament writers, can we realize its full significance. The Roman cross was doubtless the most painful and shameful instrument of execution ever devised. First invented by the Phoenicians around 600 B.C., it was adopted by the Egyptians, who passed it on to the Romans. The Romans refined the method and used it to execute runaway slaves and the worst class of criminals. But to the Jews, the cross meant something altogether different than it did to the Romans. Something that gives significance to their demand that Christ be crucified.

According to John 19:5-7, the Jews insisted that Christ be crucified because "he made himself the Son of God" (verse 7). However, when we examine the penalty prescribed for blasphemy in the Old Testament, we discover that the law stipulated death by stoning, not crucifixion (see Leviticus 24:16). Weren't the Jews in Pilate's courtyard aware of this? They certainly were. Earlier, when Christ declared, "I and my Father are one," the Jews "took up stones again to stone him" (John 10:30, 31). Why, then, did they demand that Pilate crucify Him, especially when crucifixion was not practiced by the Jews?

The answer is that they had more in mind than merely putting Christ to death. The Jews equated crucifixion with hanging on a tree, which to them meant that the person so executed was under the irrevocable curse of God (see Deuteronomy 21:23). For them, this was the same as the second death, eternal death, for remember that the Jews did not believe in the immortality of the human soul.

A good example of the Jews' idea that hanging someone on a tree represented God's eternal curse is found in the book of Joshua. God had told Abraham that He would give the Amorites (an ancient term for the Canaanites) four hundred years' probation in which to accept Him. During this time, Abraham's descendants would be slaves in Egypt (see Genesis 15:13-16). When Joshua was leading the Jews into Canaan at the end of this probationary period, five Canaanite kings joined forces to attack him. God gave Joshua the victory, and when the five kings were captured, Joshua killed them and had them hanged on five trees as evidence of God's eternal curse on those who knowingly and deliberately reject Him (see Joshua 10:25-27.)

So, to the Jews, Christ being crucified meant much more than mere physical death. It meant that He was cursed by God, the equivalent of the second death (see Isaiah 53:4, 10.) The curse of God did indeed rest upon Christ at the cross, but not because of blasphemy, as the Jews accused Him. Christ suffered the second death because God "spared not his own Son but delivered him up [to the full wages of sin] for us all" (Romans 8:32). Therefore, "Christ hath redeemed us from the curse of the law, being made a curse for us: for it is written, Cursed is every one that hangeth on a tree" (Galatians 3:13).

At this point, the question arises, "How could Christ possibly experience the second death, since He was divine?" Besides, He predicted His own resurrection and actually did rise from the dead. How could He experience "eternal death"?

Of course, the divinity of Christ did not die on the cross. Christ died as a man and as our Substitute. It was our corporate human life, which He assumed at the incarnation and which stood condemned, that died. Divinity is immortal and therefore cannot die either the first or the second death.

But what about His resurrection? How can we reconcile eternal death with the fact that He rose again? The answer lies in the "self-emptying" that took place at His incarnation.

When Christ, the second person of the Godhead, was made flesh and became the Son of Man, He "emptied himself," "made himself of no reputation" in order to represent the humanity He came to redeem (Philippians 2:6, 7). What did this actually involve? Clearly, in order to be our Saviour, Christ placed His entire being, along with every divine prerogative or power, entirely into the hands of the Father. He willingly, voluntarily made Himself a slave to the Father. The Father, in turn, took Christ and placed Him in the womb of Mary through the Holy Spirit (see Luke 1:26-35).

This meant that Christ still retained His divinity, but He gave up the independent use of that divinity while living on this earth as our representative and substitute. That is why the Scripture says that as a child Jesus grew in wisdom (see Luke 2:40, 52)— something that would not have been possible had He retained His divine prerogatives. As a man, He declared that He could do nothing apart from the Father (see John 5:19, 30; 6:57). He had to live on this earth as men have to live—totally dependent on God by faith alone.

Note the following comparisons between Christ as God and Christ as man:

CHRIST AS GOD	CHRIST AS MAN
1. Immortal (John 1:4; 5:26).	1. Mortal (Romans 10:5; 5:6; 1 Corinthians 15:3).
2. Creator (John 1:3; Colossians 1:16).	2. Made human (Matthew 2:1; Hebrews 2:9; 10:5).
3. Knows all things (John 2:24, 25; 16:30).	3. Must acquire knowledge (Luke 2:40, 52).
4. Independent (John 10:18).	4. Dependent (John 5:19, 30; 6:57; 8:28).

As God, all that is true of God the Father is true of Christ. Likewise, as man, all that is true of humanity was true of Christ (see Hebrews 2:14-17). Therefore, for Christ, as God, to become like us, He had to empty Himself completely of all His divine prerogatives. Only then could He be made in all points like as we are and qualify to be our Saviour and Substitute.

This throws important light on His death at the cross. As the Son of Man, Christ was dependent on His Father not only for His every need, but also for His resurrection. Even though Christ possessed His own uncreated, unborrowed, divine life, He could not raise Himself from the dead without the authority and direction of the Father. Scripture clearly teaches that Christ was raised from the dead by the glorious power of the Father (see Romans 6:4; Acts 2:24, 32; Ephesians 1:20).

Let's look again at the death of Christ on the cross—this time in the light of the truth about His dependence on His Father. We have already seen what Satan did to Christ on the cross through evil men. But besides that, and apart from it, God also did something to His beloved Son on the cross. Isaiah says that He "laid on him the iniquity of us all" (Isaiah 53:6). The wrath of God against all sin was heaped upon Christ our Sin Bearer as He hung on the cross. That is why the Bible says that God "spared not his own Son, but delivered him up for us all"

(Romans 8:32; cf. Isaiah 53:4, 10; Romans 4:25).

The sanctuary service revealed this truth when the sacrificial lamb, representing Christ, was consumed by divine fire on the altar (see Leviticus 9:24). The fire represented God's wrath against sin (see Hebrews 12:29). Christ implied this same truth when He instituted the first communion service at the Last Supper in the upper room. He took the cup and said, "Drink ye all of it; for this is my blood of the new testament, which is shed for many for the remission of sins" (Matthew 26:27, 28). Later, in the Garden of Gethsemane, we hear Him pray in agony three times, "O my Father, if it be possible, let this cup pass from me: nevertheless not as I will, but as thou wilt" (Matthew 26:39).

What did Jesus mean by "this cup"? The answer is found in the three angels' messages of Revelation 14.

> The third angel followed them, saying with a loud voice, If any man worship the beast and his image, and receive his mark in his forehead or in his hand, the same shall drink of the wine of the wrath of God, which is poured out without mixture into the cup of his indignation (verses 9, 10).

The cup is the irrevocable curse of God, the second death, eternal death.

All during His life on earth, Christ had lived by faith, depending totally upon His Father. Apart from the Father, Christ could do nothing. This was part of the price He had to pay in order to be the second Adam, the Saviour of the world. But at the cross, something terrible happened to Him. The Father abandoned Him (see Matthew 27:46)! Christ was left alone and without hope. Without the hope of the resurrection. Without the hope of ever seeing His Father again.

The eternal life Christ possessed, and which He had placed in the Father's charge at the incarnation, was now being taken from Him in order that God might give it to the fallen human race. In turn, the second death, which rightfully belonged to us, was now being experienced by our Lord (see Hebrews 2:9.) In the ultimate sense, this is what Paul meant when he said, "He [God] hath made him [Christ] to be sin for us, who knew no sin" (2 Corinthians 5:21).

This was the supreme sacrifice Christ had to make in order to save us. The Good Shepherd was laying down His life for His sheep, not for three days, but for eternity (see John 10:11, 15.) In this context, we can understand what Christ meant when He said, "For God so loved the world, that he gave [not lent] his only begotten Son" (John 3:16). When the disciples realized this clearly, it transformed them from a group of self-centered men into truly converted followers, ready to turn the world upside down with the gospel (see Acts 17:6.) This same transformation will take place in our lives when we fully realize the meaning of the cross (see 2 Corinthians 5:14, 15.)

Unseen by human eyes, Satan watched the great drama play itself out at the cross. He was aware of the issues involved. And although he was responsible for putting Christ on the cross, he didn't want to see the human race saved, nor did he want God to display His unconditional *agape* love. So while Christ was suffering incomprehensible mental anguish under the wrath of God, Satan came to Him once more with fierce temptations beyond anything we can understand. "He saved others; let him save himself, if he be Christ, the chosen of God," Satan inspired his human agents to mock. "If thou be the king of the Jews, save thyself" (Luke 23:35-37).

How can we understand such superhuman temptations? From the human point of view, Christ had every reason to save Himself and let the ungrateful world be lost. But no! Christ's love for the sinful race was greater than His love for Himself. "Hereby perceive we the love [*agape*] of God, because he laid down his life for us" (1 John 3:16). At the cross, Christ had to make a decision that would determine the destiny of the whole human race: Would He go against the will of His Father and exercise His own divine power to come down from the cross and save Himself? Or would He make a total, eternal sacrifice of Himself and save the world by submitting to the just wages of sin? This was the real issue facing Him. He could not save Himself and the world at the same time; it must be one or the other.

Christ chose to say goodbye to eternal life so that you and I could have it. In exchange, He accepted the second death, the just penalty for sin, which you and I deserve. Christ's divine life didn't end at the cross, but He laid it down for you and me in exchange for the second death that rightfully belongs to us.

He gave up His eternal life, not just for three days, but forever. This is the supreme sacrifice of the cross; this is the bitter cup Christ had to drink and that produced great drops of blood at Gethsemane as He pleaded in His humanity for the Father to release Him.

Once He made the self-sacrificing choice that as the second Adam He would accept the second death for every human being, Christ cried out, "It is finished!" (John 19:30). Then He bowed His head and died. What was finished? The sacrifice of the atonement. The price for every sin was fully paid once and for all (see Romans 6:10). While we were yet sinners and enemies of God, we were reconciled to God by the death of His Son (see Romans 5:8, 10). "God was in Christ, reconciling the world unto himself" (2 Corinthians 5:19).

In no way did Christ ever yield to sin while He was in human flesh. Therefore, He did not deserve to be punished by the second death. Although Christ chose to assume our sins and to experience the second death on our behalf, God was perfectly just in returning to Him His divine life, which He had laid aside for sinful human beings. Yet this returned life no longer belonged to Christ alone. Through His sacrifice on the cross, Christ's eternal life has become a shared life.

Before the cross, Scripture refers to Christ as "the *only* begotten of the Father" (John 1:14). The Greek word translated *only begotten* actually means "unique" or "one of a kind." After the cross, and in the resurrection, Christ becomes "the *first* begotten of the dead" (Revelation 1:5). This is an important distinction. "*Only* begotten" can apply to no one but an only child, but "*first* begotten" applies to the first among many children. This is the difference the cross has made. Before the cross, God had only one beloved Son. Now, through the supreme sacrifice of Christ on the cross, God has many beloved sons and daughters, of whom Christ is the first (see 1 John 3:1, 2; 1 Peter 1:3, 4). What a wonderful Saviour we have! Christ has become the head of a new redeemed humanity; He is the firstfruits, or firstborn, of all who are in Him (see 1 Corinthians 15:20, 23). In the resurrection, Christ, who sanctifies, and the believers who are sanctified, "are all of one" (Hebrews 2:11), that is, they share the same life.

Not only has Christ delivered us from the condemnation of sin and death, but much more, He has raised us up and made us to be the very sons and daughters of God. One day, we will share His very throne in heaven and in the earth made new (see Revelation 20:6; 22:5). No wonder Paul was lost for words when he declared, "Thanks be to God for his unspeakable gift" (2 Corinthians 9:15). No wonder Paul could glory in nothing but Christ and Him crucified (see Galatians 6:14).

Key Points in Chapter 8
The Cross and the Atonement

1. Christ's physical suffering on the cross, terrible as it was, played no part in our atonement.
2. The cross not only fully revealed Satan's malignant hatred, it also revealed the depths of God's *agape* love.
3. The wages of sin is not merely death, but the second death, which is eternal death. This is the death Christ experienced on the cross.
4. For the Jews, crucifying Christ meant more than mere physical death. It demonstrated that He was under God's curse (see Isaiah 53:4, 10; Deuteronomy 21:33).
5. Christ's divinity did not die on the cross. It was our corporate human life that He assumed at the incarnation that died the eternal death.
6. God did something to Christ on the cross—He "laid on him the iniquity of us all" (Isaiah 53:6). God's wrath against sin was heaped upon Christ as our Sin Bearer.
7. At the cross, the Father abandoned His Son, leaving Christ alone and without hope—without hope of the resurrection; without hope of ever seeing His Father again. The second death that rightfully belonged to us was placed upon Him. He gave up His eternal life forever for us.
8. Before the cross, Jesus is called the *"only-begotten* of the Father" (John 1:14), meaning "unique" or "one of a kind." After the cross and the resurrection, He is called the *"first-begotten* of the dead" (Revelation 1:5). Before the cross, God had only one beloved Son. Through the supreme sacrifice of Christ on the cross, God has many beloved sons and daughters, of whom Christ is first (see 1 John 3:1, 2; 2 Peter 1:3, 4).

Chapter Nine

The Cross and the Human Race

When we studied the "two Adams," we saw that "in Adam all die," while "in Christ shall all be made alive" (1 Corinthians 15:22). Since all of us have sinned in Adam (see Romans 5:12), then all of us must ultimately die the second death, which is the wages of that sin. Apart from the Saviour, every child of Adam is born on death row. The eternal life Christ offers us as a free gift is always in contrast to the eternal death we inherit in Adam.

> God so loved the world, that he gave his only begotten Son, that whosoever believeth in him should not perish [say goodbye to life forever], but have everlasting life (John 3:16).

Christ did not come to *change* the death sentence hanging over the human race. Rather, He came to *fulfill* that death sentence and make a way of escape for lost humanity. To change the death sentence would mean that Christ would have to break His own law or make it void. This can never be, for the law is a revelation of His just, righteous character that never changes (see Hebrews 13:8).

Since we have all sinned in Adam, we must all die. But Christ came that we may be made alive in Him. To understand this, we must go back and look again at 1 Corinthians 15:45, 47. These two verses refer to Adam as the "first Adam" and the "first man." They call Christ the "last Adam" and the "second man." According to verse 45, Adam is the first head of the human race, and Christ is the last (or second) head of the same human race. In verse 47, Adam is the head of the first, or old, human race; Christ is the head of the second, or new, human race.

As the second Adam, Christ gathered to Himself the whole human race and died the second, eternal death—the wages of sin that we all deserved in the first Adam. He arose from the dead as the second man, the head of a new humanity who are all in Him. "If any man be in Christ, he is a new creature; old things are passed away; behold, all things are become new" (2 Corinthians 5:17). At the cross, old things passed away; at the resurrection, all things became new.

Not only Christ died the second death on the cross; we, too, died in Him. Thus He forever delivered us from our doomed situation in Adam. Through His resurrection, we were made alive in Him, born anew to a "lively hope" (1 Peter 1:3) that is entirely of grace. Christ, the second man, stands as the head of a new humanity. This is the truth we all confess and submit to when we are baptized into Christ (see Romans 5:3-6). Baptism is simply our surrender to what God did to us in Christ's death, burial, and resurrection.

Through the cross, we have said goodbye forever to the life we inherited in Adam. In exchange, we have received the life of Christ. This truth, above any other, will determine whether we remain carnal Christians, living like ordinary men and women (see 1 Corinthians 3:1-3), or become spiritual Christians bearing the fruit of Christ's life (see John 15:4-8).

The whole human race, which originated in the first Adam, died in Christ, the last Adam. This is a necessity, because without first doing away with us in Adam, Christ could not introduce us into the new human race to which we have been born in Him. The following texts make it clear from Scripture that Christ's cross was a corporate cross on which the whole human race died in order that we might be set free from the rule of sin and the devil and be made alive to God:

I have been put to death with Christ on his cross, so that it is no longer I who live, but it is Christ who lives in me (Galatians 2:19, 20, TEV).

You have died, and your life is hidden with Christ in God (Colossians 3:3, TEV).

We are ruled by the love of Christ, now that we recognize that one man died for everyone, which means that they all share in his death (2 Corinthians 5:14, TEV).

This is a true saying: "If we have died with him, we shall also live with him" (2 Timothy 2:11, TEV).

Conclusion

In the last three chapters we have looked at three great truths about the cross. We may summarize them as follows:

1. Satan's true character, along with the true nature of sin and the sinful world, was revealed at the cross when the Son of God was put to open shame, subjected to incomprehensible suffering, and brutally crucified.

2. In contrast, the cross fully displayed God's love and justice when Christ bore the full guilt and penalty of sin on behalf of the entire human race. He thus experienced the second, or eternal, death for every person—"the just for the unjust" (1 Peter 3:18).

3. The whole human race was included in Christ, the last Adam, so that every man and woman died in Him on the cross. In Christ, we all paid the penalty for sin required by the law and were forever delivered from the power and condemnation of sin that was our situation in Adam.

Therefore, the cross of Christ becomes the means by which we:

1. gain a true knowledge of sin and the devil;

2. receive forgiveness of our sins because Christ bore the guilt and penalty of all sins;

3. experience the power of God over sin because He has struck a death blow to our life of sin. In exchange, God gives us the very life of Christ that has conquered sin in the flesh (see Romans 8:3).

Key Points in Chapter 9
The Cross and the Human Race

1. Not only Christ died the second death on the cross; we, too, died in Him. As the second Adam, Christ gathered to Himself the whole human race and died the second, eternal, death. He arose from the dead as the second man, the head of a new humanity who are all in Him.

2. The cross of Christ was a corporate cross on which the whole human race died in order that we might be set free from the rule of sin and be made alive to God.

3. The cross of Christ becomes the means by which we:
   a. gain a true knowledge of sin and the devil;
   b. receive forgiveness of our sins because Christ bore the guilt and penalty of all sins;
   c. experience the power of God over sin.

Chapter Ten

Righteousness by Faith

In chapter 3, we defined the gospel and salvation as an objective fact. We saw that in Christ, all humanity has obtained full and complete salvation because Christ's life has provided salvation from sin's guilt and punishment, its power, and its curse (see Ephesians 2:5, 6).

In this chapter, we will turn our attention to the *subjective* aspect of the gospel—salvation as a personal experience. What God has prepared and provided in Christ for all mankind (the objective gospel) must become real in our experience (the subjective gospel) if it is to be of value to us. The objective gospel can become a reality to us only when we experience its power in our lives. Not only did Jesus say that we shall know the truth, but He also added, "The truth shall make you free" (John 8:32). The truth can make us free only when we believe and receive it in our hearts (see Mark 16:15, 16; Romans 5:17). Until that happens, the truth remains a mere theory to us.

When we studied the objective gospel, we looked at salvation from God's point of view. When we study the subjective gospel, we look at salvation from humanity's point of view. From God's perspective, we are saved by grace (see Ephesians 2:8, 9), and Christ is our righteousness. From the human-response perspective, we are saved by faith, and the righteousness of Christ becomes ours by faith alone. In other words, the subjective gospel is making real in our experience the objective facts of the gospel. *Faith* is the key word in the subjective gospel, and we need to look at this word in detail.

Genuine faith

Faith is our human response to the objective facts of the gospel. In order to be genuine faith, this response must always be motivated by love, a heart appreciation of the gospel. John 3:14-16 makes it clear that faith is our heartfelt response to God's love expressed in the gift of Jesus Christ and Him crucified. Once we understand the objective facts of the gospel, especially the truth concerning the cross, then "the love of Christ constraineth us; because we thus judge, that if one died for all, then were all dead: And that he died for all, that they which live should not henceforth live unto themselves, but unto him which died for them, and rose again" (2 Corinthians 5:14, 15). The fact that Christ was willing to say goodbye to His eternal life forever so that we might live can fill us only with love and adoration. This is genuine faith that works by love (see Galatians 5:6) and produces genuine worship.

Satan, the great enemy of our souls, has prepared at least one counterfeit for every objective truth of the gospel. His counterfeit for Christ's righteousness, for example, is self-righteousness. Self-righteousness may look good; it may even appear to be genuine righteousness, but it is not of the gospel and therefore is like filthy rags in God's eyes (see Romans 10:3, 4; Isaiah 64:6).

Satan's counterfeit for genuine faith is an egocentric faith motivated by self-interest. Like the genuine article, this counterfeit faith professes to be in Christ, but it originates from our sinful human natures, which are dominated by concern for self. Because it does not belong to the gospel of Christ, it has no power to produce good works.

In contrast to this egocentric faith, the everlasting gospel of the three angels' messages offers us the faith of Jesus, which is able to produce in us the patience of the saints and enable us to keep the commandments of God (see Revelation 14:12). "The faith of Jesus" is the faith He demonstrated during His earthly life and by which He was victorious on the cross. It is described in the Laodicean message as "gold tried in the fire" (Revelation 3:18; cf.

1 Peter 1:7). Because Jesus' faith was motivated by *agape* love, it was able to withstand even the fiery test of the second death.

The first thing, then, that we must understand about genuine faith is that it is our human response to the gospel, and it is always motivated by love, a deep, heartfelt appreciation of Christ.

One reason why so many Christians today fail to demonstrate the power of the gospel in their lives is that their faith is a self-centered faith. It is self-centered because they have failed to understand the facts of the objective gospel—Christ our righteousness. If a person does not believe that full and complete salvation has already been obtained in Jesus Christ, if a person believes that salvation ultimately depends to some degree on his or her behavior, then the faith such a person is able to generate will naturally be polluted with self-concern.

Where justification by faith is not clearly understood, there is insecurity. Where there is insecurity, there is fear. And where there is fear, there can be no real love—only concern for self. "Perfect love casteth out fear: because fear hath torment [of the judgment]" (1 John 4:18).

The idea that "I have to be good," or "I'm not good enough to qualify for heaven" is one of the great stumbling blocks hindering God's people today from experiencing genuine faith. As a result, the church is spiritually bankrupt (see Revelation 3:17). That is why it is so tremendously important that we understand the objective facts of the gospel, the truth as it is in Jesus. Without this understanding, we can never experience genuine faith that is motivated by love (see Galatians 5:6).

Saving faith

Genuine faith must be motivated by love, but it must also be a saving faith. What is saving faith?

It is *not* simply trusting Christ.

Too many Christians trust Christ for salvation in the same way they trust their insurance company for material security. Such a faith is founded on self-interest and is, therefore, a counterfeit to saving faith. Although saving faith includes absolute trust in God, it involves much more. True saving faith is motivated by love and always includes three important elements: (1) knowing the truth as it is in Jesus; (2) believing the truth as it is in Jesus; and (3) obeying the truth as it is in Jesus. Let's look briefly at each of these elements.

1. *Knowing the truth.* Many texts in Scripture plainly teach that a knowledge of the gospel is a necessary and essential element to having a saving faith. The apostle Paul made it clear that faith comes by hearing, and hearing by the Word of God (see Romans 10:17). The context of his statement indicates that the source of faith is hearing the gospel of peace, the truth as it is in Jesus. Christ Himself declared that knowing Him is essential to saving faith. "Ye shall know the truth, and the truth shall make you free. . . . If the Son therefore shall make you free, ye shall be free indeed" (John 8:32, 36). He also said in prayer to the Father, "This is life eternal, that they might know thee the only true God, and Jesus Christ, whom thou hast sent" (John 17:3).

The heart of the Jewish problem in the New Testament was that they did not understand the gospel. "I bear them record," said Paul, "that they have a zeal of God, but not according to knowledge. For they being ignorant of God's righteousness, and going about to establish their own righteousness, have not submitted themselves unto the righteousness of God" (Romans 10:2, 3).

Because knowing the gospel is essential, Jesus gave this great commission to His disciples, "Go ye into all the world, and preach the gospel to every creature" (Mark 16:15). This is why He said, "This gospel of the kingdom shall be preached in all the world for a witness unto all nations; and then shall the end come" (Matthew 24:14; cf. Revelation 14:6). We must earnestly seek to know more fully the truth as it is in Jesus, because the knowledge of the gospel is a saving knowledge that will increase and deepen our faith (see Ephesians 4:11-15).

2. *Believing the truth.* The Bible is clear that a mere head knowledge of the truth does not save. True saving faith must include *believing* the truth. "He that believeth [the gospel] and is baptized shall be saved" (Mark 16:16). In Greek, the words *faith* and *belief* come from the same root word because faith always involves belief. Not only must a person mentally believe the gospel; this belief must also come from the heart.

Paul told the Roman Christians, "Your faith is spoken of throughout the whole world" (Romans 1:8). What made their faith outstanding? The answer is found in Romans 6:17, "God be thanked, that . . . ye have obeyed *from the heart* that form of doctrine [the gospel] which was delivered you" (emphasis supplied).

In the parable of the sower (see Matthew 13:3-9, 15, 18-23), Christ illustrated many kinds of believers who respond to the Word, but the only ones whose faith is of value and bears fruit are those who understand the gospel and make a heart response to it (see verse 23; cf. Acts 8:36-38). A person may respond positively to the gospel for many reasons. Some, especially in the third world, may respond to the gospel in order to gain free or inexpensive education, a job, clothes, or food.

Others may join the church because of family pressure, emotional security, etc. But such a response is not genuine faith; it will never be able to bear good fruit or stand the test of trial. Only those whose faith is founded on a heartfelt response to gospel truth have genuine saving faith.

3. *Obeying the truth.* Third, saving faith involves total submission to the objective facts of the gospel. Above all, this is the element that makes faith an instrument by which we can experience the power of the gospel.

Unfortunately, here is where many go wrong. Genuine saving faith must go beyond a mere mental assent to the gospel. James warned, "Thou believest that there is one God; thou doest well: the devils also believe, and tremble" (James 2:19). Obedience to the truth is the evidence of our faith.

As we study the objective facts of the gospel, we discover many things about ourselves that were realized in Christ's doing and dying. For example, we discover that when Christ died to sin on the cross, we also died there *in Him*. Thus a saving faith means that we will identify ourselves with that fact; we will realize that we, too, must say goodbye forever to our old life of sin that we inherited in Adam. Only then will we be qualified to be resurrected and live with Christ (see Romans 6:8; 2 Timothy 2:11). Genuine saving faith requires us to surrender ourselves to all the facts of Christ and Him crucified.

We all know that when we believe, we do not die to sin personally, in and of ourselves. We still possess the old sinful nature. Consequently, we are totally unable to live the life God demands even though we are Christian believers. Christ must live in us, and the thing that motivates us to allow Him to do so is knowing, and submitting to, the truth that when He died, our natural, sinful life was put to death *in Him*. Paul points to this as the secret of his experience: "I am crucified with Christ: nevertheless I live; yet not I, but Christ liveth in me: and the life which I now live in the flesh I live by the faith [total surrender] of the Son of God, who loved me, and gave himself for me" (Galatians 2:20).

"Reckon [or consider] ye also yourselves to be dead indeed unto sin," Paul counsels the Roman Christians, "but alive unto God through Jesus Christ our Lord" (Romans 6:11). When we live on this plane of faith, our old life is no longer in control, since it is crucified with Christ; the resurrected life of Christ dominates through the indwelling Spirit. Such a life is pleasing to God (see Galatians 5:22-24; John 15:4-8).

To live by faith alone means, above all else, to live a life that is totally surrendered to Christ as our righteousness. Faith then becomes a channel of saving power through which we stand justified and by which Christ's character is reproduced in us. In this way, Christ's righteousness becomes our personal experience by faith. This is what it means to walk in the Spirit (see Galatians 5:16, 17; 2 Corinthians 3:17, 18).

Saving faith, therefore, involves much more than simply trusting in Christ for eternal security. It means much more than simply depending on Christ to help us keep the law or "be good." God will never help the flesh to be good, for the flesh is Satan's domain and unalterably opposed to God (see Romans 8:7; Galatians 5:17). The formula for successful Christian living is always "Not I, but Christ." Saving faith demands that we maintain a humble attitude of complete surrender to the reality that when Christ was crucified, we were crucified *in Christ*. He, not self, must live in us and manifest Himself through us.

Active faith, understood and practiced, amounts to following Jesus' advice, "Watch and pray, that ye enter not into temptation" (Matthew 26:41), or "Pray without ceasing" (1 Thessalonians 5:17). This is how we live by faith alone.

Thus not only do we stand justified by faith alone, but we are sanctified by faith alone as well. The moment we step off the platform of faith alone, the flesh immediately takes over, and we are overcome by sin. Like Paul, we find ourselves doing the very opposite of the good we want to do (see Romans 7:15-24). Righteousness by faith, therefore, includes both the joy of justification as well as the experience of sanctification.

The role of faith

Some Christians believe and teach that our faith saves us. This is not true. Faith, in and of itself, can save no one. Nowhere does the Bible say that we are saved *because of* our faith or *on account of* our faith. If faith saves us, then it becomes a form of works that we can boast about. I can say, "I am saved because I believe in Christ. I have *done* something!"

The Bible teaches that we are saved *by* faith or *through* faith. Faith is only the instrument or channel by which we receive Christ as our righteousness. It is Christ—His life, His death, His resurrection—that saves us, nothing else.

The function of faith is to unite us to Christ. A tow bar unites a broken-down automobile to a wrecker. The disabled car has no ability to move on its own; the wrecker has great power. Faith, like the tow bar, unites us, who are dead in sins and who can do nothing righteous on our own, to Christ, who has conquered, condemned, and triumphed over sin in the flesh (see Romans 3:10-12; 8:3; Ephesians 2:1, 5).

Jesus said, "Without me ye can do nothing" (John 15:5). But Paul said, "I can do all things through Christ which strengtheneth me" (Philippians 4:13). All power belongs to Christ, who is able to save us to the uttermost. Through faith, Christ can produce in us the very righteousness of God (see Romans 8:4; Hebrews 7:25; Revelation 14:12).

Faith must always have an object; our faith must be in someone or something. And the object of genuine faith is always Christ. Nothing must take His place, not even our faith. By faith we become one with Christ so that His righteousness is counted as our righteousness; His power is made available to us. This is what it means to be standing in grace (see Romans 5:2).

Faith is God's gift; it is not something we have or can generate ourselves (see Romans 12:3). The gospel is foolishness to the natural mind (see 1 Corinthians 2:14), so how can a person produce faith in and of himself to believe and accept it? He cannot, without the Holy Spirit.

To be saved by faith means that we rest entirely on Christ and His righteousness—both for our standing before God in the judgment and also for our personal, day-by-day Christian experience. This is the foundation upon which the doctrine of righteousness by faith rests (see Philippians 3:9-11).

Works of faith

It's important to understand the difference between "works of faith" and "works of the law." Works of faith genuinely belong to the gospel, indeed, are a necessary fruit of it, but works of the law are a subtle counterfeit of the devil.

Anyone who has a true saving faith in Christ will also manifest in his or her behavior the indwelling life of Christ. The Bible calls this life of Christ that lives in us "the fruit of the Spirit" (Galatians 5:22). The apostle James identifies these fruits as works of faith (see 2:14-26).

According to James, many Christians in his day thought of faith as a mere mental assent to the gospel—an attitude that is still prevalent today, unfortunately. In correcting this false view of faith, James argues that faith involves more than a superficial, self-centered acceptance of the gospel. He makes it clear that without works, faith is dead (see James 2:17, 20, 26). Faith must manifest itself in our lives; otherwise, we really don't have faith at all. True faith, then, is dynamic. It unites us with Christ, and therefore must produce in our lives the works of Christ—His righteousness—through the indwelling Spirit of Christ (see 2 Corinthians 3:17, 18).

How does all this differ from the "works of the law" that Paul so earnestly opposes in his letters? (See Romans 3:20; 9:30-33; Galatians 2:16; Ephesians 2:8, 9.) Paul is not contradicting James; the two inspired writers are in full agreement, since Paul, too, upholds works of faith (see Ephesians 2:10; Titus 2:7, 14; 3:8; Hebrews 10:24).

The New Testament writers did not have a Greek word equivalent to our word *legalism*. Instead, they used the phrase "works of law" to mean the same thing. The difference between "works of law" and "works of faith," between legalism and the obedience that results from faith, is subtle because it doesn't lie primarily in the works themselves. The difference is in the *source* or *origin* of these works. For example, works of faith mean that God's law or will is being fulfilled in the life. However, works of law *appear* externally to be legitimate commandment keeping also. Both are concerned to do God's will as expressed in His law. On the surface, there seems to be no difference. Only when we look deeply enough to discover the *motivation* behind the works do we recognize that there is a great difference between "works of faith" and "works of law."

Works of faith originate from the indwelling life of Christ; works of law always originate from the flesh, the natural life. In works of faith, the believer is living by faith alone; in works of law, the sinner attempts to keep the law through a concern for self. He may pray to Christ for help, or even plead with God for the power of the Holy Spirit, but at the center of all his works and effort is only the natural strength of the flesh. This was the heart of the problem in the Galatian church. The Christians there had been born of the Holy Spirit; that is, they had received the life of Christ. But Satan had deceived them into trying to perfect their characters through the flesh (see Galatians 3:1-3). Sad to say, many of God's people today have fallen into the same subtle trap of Satan.

The formula of the gospel is "Not I, but Christ." Where there are works of faith, you will find no dependence on the energy of the flesh or the natural strength. "Works of faith" simply means Christ living in the believer's life through faith (see Galatians 2:20). Love is always the motivating factor behind all such works, because Christ is love. Therefore, love (Christ's *agape* in us) becomes the fulfillment of the law (see Romans 13:8-10; Galatians 5:14; 1 John 4:7, 12).

On the other hand, works of law always originate from a concern with self; they are therefore always polluted by self no matter how good they may appear to ourselves or to others. Performing works of law is a subtle form of rebellion against God because all such works are actually independent of Him. In the judgment, God will condemn all such works as iniquity, works motivated from self-interest (see Matthew 7:21-23; Luke 13:25-28).

Under no circumstances will God enter into partnership with the flesh (our concern for self). The flesh belongs to Satan, and therefore must be crucified (see Galatians 5:24). When we give up all confidence in the flesh and live by faith alone, then God can produce godliness—genuine righteousness—in us. And He will do so. God did not give us His only-begotten Son so that we could *copy* Him, but so that we could *receive* Him.

Our lives will become pleasing to God only as we completely surrender ourselves to Him who loved us and gave Himself for us (see John 15:1-8). God is not looking at us to see how good we are or how hard we are trying to keep His law. There is only one thing that God looks for in each of us—how much of His Son Jesus does He see in us?

Key Points in Chapter 10
Righteousness by Faith

1. The subjective aspect of the gospel is our personal experience of salvation. What God has done for all mankind in Christ (the objective gospel) must become real in our experience (the subjective gospel) if it is to be of value to us.

2. From God's perspective, we are saved by grace, and Christ is our righteousness (see Ephesians 2:8, 9). From the human-response perspective we are saved by faith, and the righteousness of Christ becomes ours by faith alone.

3. In order to be genuine, faith must always be motivated by love, a heart appreciation of the gospel. Satan's counterfeit to genuine faith is an egocentric faith motivated by self-interest.

4. Saving faith includes three important elements:
   a. Knowing the truth.
   b. Believing the truth.
   c. Obeying the truth.

5. Not only do we stand justified by faith alone, but we are sanctified by faith alone as well.

6. The role of faith is to unite us to Christ. We are not saved *because* of our faith; we are saved *by* faith. Faith is the channel by which we receive Christ's righteousness. He saves us.

7. Anyone who has true saving faith in Christ will also manifest the indwelling life of Christ in his/her behavior. This behavior will exhibit "works of faith."

8. "Works of law," on the other hand, originate from the flesh—not from the indwelling life of Christ. "Works of law" and "works of faith" may appear the same on the surface; the difference is their source and motivation.

Chapter Eleven

Justification and Sanctification

Now that we have defined genuine saving faith and have seen what role it plays in our salvation, let's look at the two main areas—justification and sanctification—that together make up this doctrine of righteousness by faith. There is much confusion in the church today over these aspects of righteousness by faith.

To begin with, we must be clear on two points. First, both justification and sanctification are founded upon the objective gospel—what Christ by His holy history has already prepared and provided for the fallen human race. Second, it is by faith alone that we receive and experience both justification and sanctification.

What do we really mean by these terms—justification and sanctification? What is involved in each, and how do they differ from each other?

Keeping in mind that both are founded on the objective facts of the gospel, we may describe justification as the righteousness of Christ that is *imputed*, or credited, to us as a consequence of accepting Christ by faith. Sanctification is the righteousness of Christ that is *imparted*, or given, to us as a result of living by faith.

The legal justification effected at the cross is not something we experience; it is something we receive as a free gift. Sanctification, on the other hand, is something we personally experience as we walk by faith. In both cases, the thing that we receive and experience is the righteousness of Christ. Therefore, justification is the gift of the gospel that legally declares us righteous before God, while sanctification is the provision of the gospel that actually produces righteousness in us. The one qualifies us for heaven; the other makes us fit to live in heaven. Thus the gospel fully satisfies all our needs.

In chapter 3, we saw that justification is simply the objective gospel applied to the believer who has put on Christ by faith. In other words, when a person accepts the gospel and is united by faith to Christ, immediately all that Christ has prepared and provided as humanity's substitute is made effective for that person. The history of Christ now becomes lawfully the history of the believer because he is in Christ by faith. God looks at such a person as being perfect in obedience, justice, and nature, since all three were obtained for him in the holy history of Christ.

Such a person is no longer under condemnation; he has passed from death to life (see John 5:24; Romans 8:1). God looks at the justified believer as if he has met *all* the demands necessary to qualify for heaven and eternal life. Justification, then, is the work of a moment—a heart response to what Christ has already accomplished.

Sanctification, by contrast, is an hourly, daily experience that continues throughout the lifetime of the believer who continues to walk by faith. The gospel not only freely gives us the righteousness of Christ in order to deliver us from the condemnation of the law; it gives us the righteousness of Christ as a personal experience so that we can reflect His character.

Anyone, therefore, who stops with justification and makes it the entire gospel experience has received only half of the good news. God did not send His Son merely to legally deliver us from sin so that He could *declare* us righteous. He sent His Son in order to also *set us free* from sin and restore His image in us. This work of restoration includes sanctification, and it, too, is part and parcel of the good news of the gospel.

It is God's purpose that the church, His people, reflect the character of their head, Jesus Christ (see Ephesians 4:11-15). This is the only way God can demonstrate to a lost world His Son's power to destroy sin and the devil. Only by putting together justification by faith (the *receiving* of Christ's righteousness) and sanctification by faith (the *experiencing* of His righteousness) do we get a complete, accurate picture of what righteousness by faith really is.

Let's summarize, then, the main differences between justification by faith and sanctification by faith:

1. Justification makes effective our legal standing before God; sanctification has to do with our daily personal experience as Christians.

2. Justification is *meritorious*; it qualifies us for heaven now and in the judgment. Sanctification is *demonstrative*; it progressively manifests in our lives what we have already been declared to be in Christ.

3. Justification is the work of a moment, although it remains effective all our believing lives. Sanctification is a lifelong work that has to be experienced daily through a living faith.

Apart from these three differences, justification and sanctification are closely related. We may separate them for purposes of discussion, but in real-life experience they are inseparable because the righteousness of Christ is the key factor in both, and we realize both by faith alone.Therefore, in its broadest sense, justification by faith includes the experience of sanctification by faith—or holy living. Note, for example, James's argument in James 2:21-24.

Common misunderstandings

Before concluding this chapter, we should look at some common misunderstandings about this important subject.

1. *Justification by faith refers only to the forgiveness of past sins.* It's true that one important truth about justification is the forgiveness of our past sins, but justification involves far more than that. The righteousness of Christ includes the fact that He endured the just penalty of the law on behalf of our sins, past, present, and future. But in a positive sense, Christ also kept the whole law on our behalf. All this becomes ours the moment we are justified by faith.

Justification means *all* of Christ's righteousness that He provided for us so that nothing more is required of us to qualify for heaven. In other words, we stand perfect in Him. If we are not absolutely clear on this point, we will continue to be victims of self-concern, constantly fearful about our eternal security. In this condition it is impossible to have a real heart appreciation for Christ's cross or to experience genuine sanctification by faith.

Forgiveness is the most wonderful thing for us sinners. But glorious as it is, forgiveness is still a negative thing, for it is concerned only with acquitting us of our sins. Justification, on the other hand, is both a negative and a positive truth. It includes the negative aspect—forgiveness—but it goes beyond that to declare us righteous and to change our hearts from being self-centered to being Christ-centered (see Philippians 1:21). The very righteousness of Christ is put to our account so that we stand before God and His law perfectly righteous—both now and in the judgment. This is the superabundant gift of the gospel (see Isaiah 54:17; Acts 13:39; Romans 10:4).

The devil has deceived many Christians into believing that justification by faith does not fully qualify them for heaven—that something more is necessary, that they must keep the law and do good works. As a result, many sincere Christians are trapped in a subtle form of legalism, living in fear and insecurity.

2. *Every time we fall or sin we become unjustified.* This is another common misunderstanding about justification. It is a monstrous teaching that has no support from the Word of God.

It's true that every time we fall into sin we misrepresent Christ and hurt Him, because even the smallest sin figured in what happened at the cross. However, God does not reject us every time we make a mistake or fall into sin. If we believe that we lose our justification in Christ each time we sin, we completely invalidate the truth of justification by faith. Such a concept is based on the idea that we are justified because of our obedience—what Christ is doing in us—and not because of what He has already accomplished for us by His doing and dying on the cross. Such an idea makes the gospel good advice instead of good news. We will look at this idea in more detail in a later chapter.

3. *It takes a lifetime or more to reach the goal of sanctification.* This is how many interpret the familiar expression, "Sanctification is the work of a lifetime." Satan is pleased to have us believe this error. On the contrary, Christians who are *not* living a Christ-filled life are living subnormally as far as the gospel is concerned. The apostle Paul rebuked the Corinthian Christians for still remaining babes in Christ only a few years after they had been

converted from rank paganism (see 1 Corinthians 3:1-3). The normal Christian life is Christ living in the heart by faith. Anything short of this is falling short of God's ideal for each believer. Such a life, of course, is possible only as we continuously believe, watch, and pray, because the sinful flesh is still very much alive and is constantly trying to assert itself. This is why sanctification is the work of a lifetime. So also is eating the work of a lifetime if we are to maintain physical life. If Christ is to continually live through and in us, the work of sanctification will be with us throughout our lifetime.

Conclusion

This, then, is what righteousness by faith is all about; it is making real in our lives the righteousness of Christ by faith. "In Christ" we are perfect and complete in every respect—in character, in performance, in nature, and legally (see Colossians 2:10). This is what God has obtained for us by His life, death, and resurrection (see Hebrews 9:12). But in actual practice, we often fall short of perfection. So the Christian life of sanctification is the experience of becoming in character what we already are "in Christ" through justification by faith. The following texts compare our standing "in Christ" (justification) with the corresponding life we then follow by faith (sanctification).

JUSTIFICATION	SANCTIFICATION
What our standing is in Christ by faith:	What our experience becomes in Christ by faith:
1. Dead to sin (Romans 6:2-10; Colossians 2:10).	1. Give no place to sin (Romans 6:11-15; 13:14; Colossians 3:1-3; 1 Peter 2:24).
2. Alive to God (John 5:24; 20:31; Romans 6:11; 8:10; 1 John 5:1).	2. Live unto God (Romans 14:8; 2 Corinthians 5:15; Galatians 2:19, 20; Titus 2:12).

3. Legally righteous
   (Romans 1:17; 3:21-26;
   4:1, 6; 5:17;
   1 Corinthians 1:30;
   Philippians 3:9).

3. Live righteously
   (2 Timothy 2:22;
   1 John 3:7;
   1 Corinthians 15:34;
   Philippians 1:11;
   1 Timothy 6:11).

4. Adopted as children of God
   (Ephesians 1:5;
   Galatians 3:26;
   1 John 3:1;
   Romans 8:16).

4. Act like God's children
   (Ephesians 5:1, 8;
   1 Peter 1:13, 14).

5. God's claimed possession
   (Ephesians 1:4;
   2 Timothy 2:19).

5. Yield or surrender to God
   (Romans 12:1;
   2 Timothy 2:19-21).

6. Not of this world, but
   citizens of heaven
   (John 15:19; 17:14-16;
   1 John 5:19).

6. Love not the world, but
   live like citizens of heaven
   (1 John 5:4, 5; 2:15;
   Colossians 3:1, 2;
   James 1:27).

7. Crucified to the world
   (Galatians 1:4; 6:14, 15).

7. Avoid worldly practices
   (1 John 2:15-17;
   James 1:27; 4:4;
   Romans 12:2).

8. Slaves of God
   (1 Corinthians 7:22, 23;
   Romans 6:22).

8. Serve joyfully as God's
   slaves
   (Romans 6:17-19;
   12:11; Hebrews 12:28).

9. Have new life
   (2 Corinthians 5:17;
   2 Peter 1:14;
   Galatians 6:15.

9. Walk in newness of life
   (Romans 6:4; 7:6;
   Ephesians 4:24).

10. Made obedient to the law
(Romans 10:4; 3:31;
Philippians 3:9).

10. Keep fulfilling the law
(Romans 8:4;
1 John 5:2, 3;
Revelation 14:12).

11. Light to the world
(Matthew 5:14;
1 Thessalonians 5:5).

11. Walk as children of light
(Matthew 5:15, 16;
Ephesians 5:8).

12. Cleansed
(John 15:3;
1 John 1:7, 9).

12. Cleanse yourselves
(2 Corinthians 7:1;
Philippians 4:8).

13. Made holy
(Ephesians 1:4;
1 Corinthians 3:17;
Hebrews 3:1).

13. Live holy lives
(1 John 3:7;
1 Peter 1:15, 16;
2 Peter 3:14).

14. Free from sin's slavery
(John 8:32-36;
Romans 6:18; 8:2).

14. Do not let sin rule you
(Romans 6:22;
Galatians 5:1, 13, 14;
2 Corinthians 3:17, 18).

15. Made secure in Christ
(1 Peter 1:5;
Romans 8:1;
John 10:27, 28).

15. Enjoy that security
(2 Peter 1:10;
Hebrews 10:19-22;
1 Thessalonians 1:5).

16. Spirit indwelt and led
(1 Corinthians 3:16; 6:19, 20;
2 Corinthians 6:16;
Romans 8:9, 10).

16. Yield to Spirit's control
(Galatians 5:16, 17, 25;
Ephesians 4:30; 5:18;
1 Thessalonians 5:19).

17. Spirit gifted
(Romans 12:5, 6;
1 Corinthians 12:4, 12;
Ephesians 4:7-13).

17. Use your gift
(Romans 12:3-8;
1 Peter 4:11).

18. Empowered for witnessing
(Luke 24:49;
Acts 1:8; 2 Corinthians 4:7;
Ephesians 3:20;
2 Timothy 1:7).

18. Witness to that power
(1 Corinthians 2:4;
Ephesians 6:10;
Philippians 3:10; 4:13).

19. Given possession of
Christ's love
(Romans 5:5;
1 Corinthians 12:31; 13:1-13;
1 John 2:5; 5:1).

19. Love as Christ loved
(John 13:34, 35;
1 Peter 1:22; 4:8;
1 John 3:18, 23;
4:7, 12).

20. Legally "in Christ"
(1 Corinthians 1:30;
Ephesians 1:3-6, 10;
2:5, 6, 13).

20. Joyfully abide in Christ
(John 15:4-7;
1 John 2:6, 28; 3:6).

The life God expects of every believer is the life of His Son. Every provision has already been made for us in Christ. We are never justified by faith *plus* works, but true justification by faith always *produces* works (see John 14:12; Ephesians 2:8-10; Titus 3:5, 8). "Whatsoever is born of God overcometh the world; and this is the victory that overcometh the world, even our faith" (1 John 5:4).

Key Points in Chapter 11
Justification and Sanctification

1. Both justification and sanctification are founded on the objective gospel—what Christ has already prepared and done for the entire human race.

2. It is by faith alone that we receive and experience both justification and sanctification.

3. Justification is the gift of the gospel that legally declares us righteous before God; sanctification is the provision of the gospel that actually produces righteousness in us.

4. Three common misunderstandings about justification and sanctification are present in the church today:

   a. *Justification by faith refers only to the forgiveness of past sins.* Justification includes forgiveness, but it goes beyond it to declare us righteous and to change our hearts from being self-centered to being Christ-centered.

   b. *Every time we fall or sin, we become unjustified.* This misunderstanding is based on the belief that our justification is based on our obedience—an idea that has no support in the Bible.

   c. *It takes a lifetime or more to reach the goal of sanctification.* Sanctification is not perfection; it is Christ living in the heart by faith—and that is the norm for Christian life. Sanctification is indeed the work of a lifetime if we are to maintain spiritual life—as is eating if we are to maintain physical life.

Chapter Twelve

The Joyous Experience of Salvation

In earlier chapters, we studied the various facets of the objective gospel—the plan of salvation that has already been prepared and provided for all humanity in Jesus Christ. In chapters 10 and 11, we saw that the truth of this gospel remains merely a set of teachings, void of power, until it becomes real in the believer's experience. In this chapter, we will examine salvation as a subjective experience. What is involved in being saved? What is the relationship between salvation as an objective fact and salvation as a subjective experience?

Salvation defined

Many look upon salvation as being delivered from death and granted eternal life, as being delivered from hell and being given heaven. Salvation does involve deliverance from death and hell, but it includes much more. When we are saved, a radical change takes place both in our position as well as our status before God.

By birth we are "in Adam." This is our natural position, and it is a hopeless one because in Adam "all have sinned" (Romans 5:12) and "all die" (1 Corinthians 15:22). However, the moment we respond sincerely to the gospel, we are delivered from our position in Adam and are united by faith to Christ. This means a radical change in position, but it also means a radical change in status.

In Adam, we belong to this world, which is totally under Satan's control and which is doomed to destruction (see John 14:30; 1 John 5:19; 2 Peter 3:9, 10). But now, being in Christ by faith, we no longer belong to this world (see John 15:19; 17:14, 16); we have been delivered from this present evil world through the cross of Christ (see Galatians 1:4). Paul says,

God forbid that I should glory, save in the cross of our Lord Jesus Christ, by whom the world is crucified unto me, and I unto the world (Galatians 6:14).

Salvation, as an *experience*, may therefore be defined as an exodus from the world, which is under Satan's control, and an entrance into the church, which is under the rule of Christ (see 1 John 5:19). The exodus of God's people from Egypt to Canaan symbolized this great truth, Egypt being a symbol of the sinful world, and Canaan representing the church destined for heaven. When Israel crossed the Red Sea (a symbol of baptism), they said goodbye forever to Egypt (the world) and Pharaoh (a symbol of Satan). When they entered Canaan, the Promised Land was a figure of the church, the realm of God (see 1 Corinthians 10:1-11).

Because of this Old Testament symbolism, the New Testament writers purposely chose the word *ecclesia* (translated *church*) to refer to the people of God. This Greek word is made up of two words—*ek*, meaning "out of" and *kaleo*, which means "to call." Thus the word *ecclesia* defines the church as "a called-out people." But from what are we, believers in Christ, called out?

The answer is that we are called out from the world. Jesus made this clear in John 15:19: "Ye are not of the world, but I have chosen you out of [*ek*] the world."

This throws important light on the experience of salvation and brings to view several implications for us as believers in Christ. First, as Christians, we no longer belong to this world; we have become citizens of heaven. Satan, "the prince of this world" (John 12:31), is at war with Christ, the Lord of heaven, so we Christians have become strangers living in enemy territory. That is why Jesus said that the world would naturally hate us and persecute us (see John 15:19; 1 John 3:13). If that is not happening, it isn't because the world has changed; it is because the world does not see Christ in us (see 2 Timothy 3:12).

Second, as citizens of heaven, all our ties to the world must come to an end. All national and racial pride must disappear, for in Christ "there is neither Jew nor Greek." All class distinctions must disappear, for "there is neither bond nor free." And even our status symbols must come to an end, for "there is neither male nor female, for ye are all one in Christ Jesus" (Galatians 3:28).

Likewise, we are to have no partnership with the world, even though we are to be in it as salt and light, seasoning and illuminating it with the good news about Jesus Christ (see Matthew 5:13, 14). James makes this clear.

> Know ye not that the friendship of the world is enmity with God? Whosoever therefore will be a friend of the world is the enemy of God (James 4:4; cf. 1:27).

Finally, to be called out of the world is to say goodbye to the root of all evil, which is "the love of money" (1 Timothy 6:10). Money is the vital ingredient that makes this world run, and the love of money is at the center of all lust. In and of itself, money is not evil; otherwise, the church could have nothing to do with it. It is *the love of money* that is the root of all evil. The love of money is synonymous with the love of self and is a clear indication that we have not let go of our self-love as the cross of Christ demands.

One good evidence that we are truly in Christ, whether rich or poor, is our relationship to money (see Matthew 6:24). For this reason, God has introduced His program of tithes and offerings (see Malachi 3:8, 9). If we are truly in Christ, returning the tithe and giving offerings will be a delight, no matter what our financial situation. On the other hand, if our faith in Christ is self-centered and not motivated by love, this will be clearly shown in our withholding tithes and offerings. Our lives will contradict Jesus' words, "It is more blessed to give than to receive" (Acts 20:35; cf. 2 Corinthians 5:7).

It is not our money that God wants; He wants us. The cross demands that we belong totally to God, for we have been bought with the precious blood of His Son (see 1 Peter 1:18, 19; 1 Corinthians 6:20; 2 Peter 2:1). How can God (or His church) know that we have truly surrendered ourselves to Him as genuine faith demands? One way is by our faithfulness in tithes and offerings. When we fail in this, we are robbing God of what is rightfully His—ourselves. One reason the church today is so financially poor is that too many members have a self-centered faith instead of a faith that works by love. Oh, that God might open our eyes to see ourselves as we truly are—"wretched and miserable, and poor, and blind, and naked" (Revelation 3:17).

Salvation and baptism

As Adventists, we sometimes focus so much on the correct *method* of baptism that we lose sight of the *significance* of this important rite. According to Jesus Himself, baptism is vitally connected to salvation. When He commissioned His disciples to preach the gospel to the whole world, He added, "He that believeth and is baptized shall be saved" (Mark 16:16).

Why did Jesus include baptism as a necessary part of salvation?

Of course, baptism itself does not save us. It is what baptism represents that is crucial. The cross of Christ stands as the great demarcation between His church and the world under Satan. Baptism is the symbol of our identification by faith with Christ's cross that separates us forever from the doomed world of sin. This is what the Bible calls being saved, or washed, by water (see 1 Corinthians 6:11; Ephesians 5:26; Titus 3:5; Revelation 1:5).

The apostle Peter draws a comparison between the waters of the Flood in Noah's day and the waters of baptism. When the Flood came, only "eight souls were saved by water," he declares, and this is an illustration of how "even baptism doth also now save us" (1 Peter 3:20, 21). In order to understand Peter's comparison, we need to ask ourselves, "From what were Noah and his family saved at the time of the Flood?" Was it not from a doomed, sinful world?

Following God's directions, Noah built the ark and preached to a lost world to enter it and be saved. But only Noah and his family, along with the animals that were on board, rode the ark in safety through the waters. Except for these eight, every living person on earth was drowned. The waters of the Flood eternally separated Noah and his family from the wicked world of which they were a part. The ark is a symbol of Christ's church. We enter His church through the waters of baptism, and this eternally separates us from the wicked world to which we belong by birth. Baptism, therefore, is the door through which we make our exit from this doomed, wicked world and enter Christ's church, which is destined for heaven.

According to Romans 6:3, 4, baptism symbolizes our union with Christ's crucifixion, burial, and resurrection. Christ died to sin and to this world (see Romans 6:10; Galatians 1:4; 6:14). So when we participate by faith in that death, we too are saying goodbye forever to sin and this wicked world. We symbolize this by our union with Him in baptism as we are buried beneath the water.

Then, just as Christ rose from the dead and left sin in the grave, so we also rise from the baptismal water to serve God in newness of life (see 2 Corinthians 5:17; Romans 6:4). Baptism becomes a public confession of our faith by which we have died with Christ and have a new life that is hidden in Him (see Colossians 3:3). Thus, the ordinance of baptism symbolizes all that our salvation involves.

Please ever keep in mind, however, that the act of baptism can never save us. The thing that saves us is our surrender to the truth that baptism represents. The Jews mistakenly came to emphasize the act of circumcision instead of its significance. We must never fall into the same error regarding baptism. Baptism, even baptism by immersion, becomes of value to us only because of what it represents—our union by faith with Christ crucified, buried, and resurrected. This is what saves us and not the act of baptism itself.

Saved into the church

The world to which we belong by birth is hostile to God and under condemnation. Therefore, in order to save us, the cross must deliver us from the world and place us in the church, the body of Christ. Every other aspect of salvation is based upon this fact. The gospel delivers us not primarily from hell to heaven, nor from death to life, but from the world to the church. As a subjective experience, this is always the first step of our salvation. *Christ will never take us to heaven as individuals, but only as members of His church.*

Now we can understand why the church on earth is Christ's supreme concern (see Ephesians 5:27). Enoch, Moses, and Elijah have already ascended to heaven, but only as the firstfruits of those who belong to the body of Christ. Jesus is preparing a place for His church and has promised to return the second time to take it to heaven. Salvation, then, begins with being delivered from the world into the church.

Tragically, we see much of the world creeping into the church today. In contradiction to the gospel of Christ, the church is copying the world's fashions, accepting its philosophy, and depending on its resources. All this is happening because the church has lost sight of the true meaning of the doctrine of salvation. No wonder the church is so weak and so indistinguishable from the world! When Christ was here on earth, He was a stranger and a pilgrim. He was in the world and witnessed to it of the truth, but He was not of the world. The same must be true of the Christian and of the church. "Whatsoever is born of God overcometh the world: and this is the victory that overcometh the world, even our faith" (1 John 5:4, 5).

To be saved means that we say goodbye to everything that belongs to the world and become a vital part of the church. The cross of Christ forbids anything that is of self or the world to cross over into the church.

The New Testament defines the church as the "body of Christ" (see Romans 12:2-5; 1 Corinthians 12:27; Ephesians 1:19-23; Colossians 1:24). When we become Christians, we become a part of that body. This is one of the things Christ had in mind when He introduced the element of the bread into the ordinance of the Lord's Supper. "We being many are one bread, and one body: for we are all partakers of that one bread" (1 Corinthians 10:17). This concept of all Christians being part of a single body—the church—has important implications for how we live as Christians. As long as we belonged to the world, we could live more or less as we pleased because the world is founded on Satan's principle of self-love. But as Christians who are vital parts of Christ's body, we can no longer live to please self. The law of the body demands that we live under the authority of the head, which is Christ (see Ephesians 5:23; Colossians 1:18). Just as the head controls the different members of the human body, so Christians must be under the full control of Christ.

The human body is perfectly coordinated because each member does nothing at all in and of itself, but operates entirely under the direction of the head. The body of Christ will likewise experience unity and perfect harmony when individual believers—members of the church—do nothing in and of themselves without living entirely under the direction of Christ, the head of the church.

Every believer, without exception, has an important function within the framework of the body. "All members have not the same office"; nevertheless, all members have a vital part to play.

> Having then gifts differing according to the grace that is given to us, whether prophecy, let us prophesy according to the proportion of faith; or ministry, let us wait on our ministering: or he that teacheth, on teaching; or he that exhorteth, on exhortation; he that giveth, let him do it with simplicity; he that ruleth, with diligence; he that sheweth mercy, with cheerfulness (Romans 12:4, 6-8; cf. 1 Corinthians 12:12-25).

This means, too, that every member will have respect for the work of other believers as well as a concern for their welfare. When the church is operating as it should, there will be no "schism in the body; but that the members should have the same care one for another. And whether one member suffer, all the members suffer with it; or one member be honoured, all the members rejoice with it" (1 Corinthians 12:25, 26).

As a human body grows and develops, so must the church. When Christ went back to heaven, He left behind special gifts for His church.

> He gave some, apostles; and some, prophets; and some, evangelists; and some, pastors and teachers, for the perfecting of the saints, for the work of the ministry, for the edifying of the body of Christ: till we all come in the unity of the faith, and of the knowledge of the Son of God, unto a perfect man, unto the measure of the stature of the fullness of Christ (Ephesians 4:11-13).

Under Satan, the world has been developing for some six thousand years. Likewise, the church must develop so that "where sin abounded, grace [must] much more abound" (Romans 5:20). The more Satan demonstrates the power of sin and self, the more must God demonstrate the power of the gospel of love through the church. Satan is a defeated foe in the great controversy between himself and Christ, but Christ's victory must be demonstrated through the church—and it will be demonstrated at the end of time.

Today, much that belongs to the world is camouflaged; even Christians are too unaware that "the whole world is in the power of the evil one" (1 John 5:19, RSV). But the time is coming and is almost here when the issues will become clearly defined. "All the world wondered after the beast. And they worshipped the dragon [the devil] which gave power unto the beast" (Revelation 13:3, 4). At that time the earth will be illuminated with the glory of God shining through His church (see Revelation 18:1). This demonstration must take place before Christ can return. The world today is indeed ripe for the end; unfortunately, the church is not. God is patiently waiting for His people to repent and seek His face with all their hearts. That is why it is so urgent that the true gospel be restored to God's people. It must become in reality "the power of God unto salvation" (Romans 1:16).

The scope of salvation

Christ came into this world to save us completely and totally from sin. How is this salvation dispensed to us who have responded positively to the good news? Many Christians have a limited understanding of the objective gospel—the salvation already prepared and finished for us in Christ Jesus. Therefore, their subjective experience of receiving this salvation is limited as well. That is why many Christians (especially Seventh-day Adventist Christians) are embarrassed when asked the simple question, "Are you saved?" In fact, those who ask the question are themselves often ignorant of the full scope of the plan of salvation.

All that is necessary for our salvation from sin is already an accomplished fact in Christ. However, as a *subjective experience*, our salvation is a past, present, and future reality. In Christ we have been saved from the guilt and punishment of sin, its power, and also its presence and its curse. This is the situation *now* with all who have submitted, by faith, to the truth as it is in Christ Jesus. But when it comes to this freedom from sin being a subjective experience in our lives, we do not receive all these aspects of salvation at the same time. All are guaranteed to the believer who is resting in Christ, but we experience them in three stages.

The first occurs at conversion, when we are united to Christ by faith. At that moment, we are saved from the guilt and punishment of sin; we are declared perfectly righteous. This is what it means to be justified. However, this does not mean that we have been saved experientially from the power or grip of sin. Freedom from the power of sin is to be something we will experience continuously, daily, as we keep on living by faith. This is the process of sanctification and will continue as long as we live.

Then at the second coming of Jesus, all believers will be saved from the curse and presence of sin. This is the "blessed hope" to which we look forward with such longing (Titus 2:13; cf. Romans 8:19-25).

So, as Christians, we may say with confidence that we *are saved*. But at the same time, we must confess that we *are being saved* and that we *will be saved*. We are already saved from all condemnation and therefore have peace with God (see Romans 5:1; 8:1), but we are also being saved from indwelling sin as we continue to "fight the good fight of faith" (1 Timothy 6:12). And finally, we look forward to Christ's glorious appearing when we shall be saved from the corruption of sin that has infiltrated every member of our bodies (see Romans 8:23-25; 1 Corinthians 15:51-57; Philippians 3:20, 21).

The full scope of salvation teaches us that our Christian hope is not limited to this life only. "If in this life only we have hope in Christ," Paul told the believers at Corinth, "we are of all men most miserable" (1 Corinthians 15:19). To stop at past salvation is to receive only one-third of the gospel. Not only must we rejoice that we have eternal life and heaven, we must allow that life to begin now. "Every man that hath this hope in him purifieth himself, even as he [God] is pure" (1 John 3:3; cf. Romans 13:14; Galatians 5:16).

Finally, we look forward to that glorious day when our Saviour will appear to take us home. There we will experience the full salvation made available to us now in Christ Jesus.

Key Points in Chapter 12
The Joyous Experience of Salvation

1. When we respond to the gospel, a radical change takes place in both our position and our status before God. "In Adam" we belonged to this world, which is controlled by Satan and doomed to destruction. "In Christ" we have become citizens of heaven and of God's church, which is controlled by Christ.

2. Baptism is a public confession of our faith by which we have died with Christ and have a new life that is hidden in Him (see Colossians 3:3).

3. Christ will never take us to heaven as individuals, but only as members of His church, which is His body.

4. We experience the full scope of our salvation in three stages:
   a. At conversion we are saved from the guilt and punishment of sin. This is justification.
   b. As we live by faith, we experience freedom from the power of sin. This is sanctification.
   c. At the second coming of Jesus, we will be saved from the curse and presence of sin. This is glorification.

5. Thus Christians can say, "I am saved"; "I am being saved"; "I will be saved." The full scope of our salvation is not limited to this life only.

Chapter Thirteen

The Principle of the Cross

Earlier in this book, we examined the cross of Christ as an objective fact. In this chapter, we will be concerned with applying this truth to our lives. The power of the gospel is based on the cross (see 1 Corinthians 1:17, 18). When the cross is applied to the life of the believer, it becomes the power of God unto salvation.

The cross also has important implications for how we live our lives as Christians. We will consider these implications before we study the cross as God's power to save from sin.

The believer's cross

Most of us are familiar with the idea that the Christian life involves bearing some type of cross (see Matthew 10:38; 16:24; Luke 9:23; 14:27). But we may not realize that this cross is none other than the cross of Christ.

The cross each Christian is called to bear is *not* the hardships and trials of this life. Many believe that God gives each believer a cross to bear—some heavy and some light. Some have to deal with very difficult circumstances, while others carry only a light cross. This idea is a deception of the devil. Jesus did not have this in mind at all when He talked about Christians bearing their cross. The hardships of life are the consequences of sin, and all people, believers and unbelievers alike, must bear them.

The cross Jesus talked about and which each believer must

carry in order to follow Him is *Jesus'* cross. In fact, it is impossible for a person to be truly united to Christ without also being identified with His cross. Baptism, as we saw in the last chapter, is the mark of our identification with Christ crucified, buried, and resurrected (see Romans 6:3-5). Faith in Christ identifies us with His cross so that it becomes our cross as well. That is why Paul says,

> God forbid that I should glory, save in the cross of our Lord Jesus Christ, by whom the world is crucified unto me, and I unto the world (Galatians 6:14; cf. Galatians 2:20).

We must never separate our cross from the cross of Christ, because there is no salvation from sin apart from His cross. When Christ was crucified, three things took place that vitally affect the life of every believer. These may be summarized as:

1. What Satan and the world did to Christ on the cross. This is the offense of the cross;

2. what God did to His Son on the cross. This involves the blood of Christ;

3. what God did for the human race in Christ on the cross. This focuses on Christ's cross itself.

We will look at each of these in turn.

The offense of the cross

The offense of the cross came because of what Satan and the world did to Christ on the cross. There they showed their absolute and utter hatred for Him. This hatred led them to put Him to an open shame (see Hebrews 6:6), inflict untold suffering on Him, and finally hang Him on the cross to die an excruciating death. The Bible refers to this truth, applied to the life of every believer, as "the offense of the cross" (Galatians 5:11).

Becoming a Christian is much more than merely joining a denomination. It involves a radical change of position and status. A person who becomes a genuine believer is no longer "in Adam," but is now "in Christ." He or she no longer belongs to the world but has become a citizen of God's kingdom. Because a great war is going on between Satan, the prince of this world, and Christ, the Lord of heaven, it is clear that anyone who says goodbye to his position in this world and unites himself with Christ's kingdom on earth (His church) is bound to be attacked by Satan and the world. Jesus warned His disciples, "If ye were of the world, the world would love his own: but because ye are not of the world, but I have chosen you out of the world, therefore the world hateth you" (John 15:19; cf. 1 John 3:13). Paul says, "Yea, and all that will live godly in Christ Jesus shall suffer persecution" (2 Timothy 3:12).

But, you say, the church is not suffering persecution today.

The church is not being persecuted today not because the world has improved, nor because a reconciliation has taken place between Christ and Satan. The church is not being persecuted today because an unholy marriage has taken place between the church and the world. The church has so long been in partnership in one form or another with the world that it is in captivity as was Israel of old in Babylon. For years, God's people have been ignoring His clear counsel and borrowing the philosophies of the world—using and depending on its resources, involving ourselves in the world's politics, having dialogues with various worldly organizations. This is most noticeable in those parts of the globe where the church works under the direction of secular governments. This is why God's final message to His church is, "Come out of her [Babylon], my people, that ye be not partakers of her sins, and that ye receive not of her plagues" (Revelation 18:4).

Although the distinction between the church and the world is hardly visible today, this condition will not continue for long. God has made it clear that He will step in and remedy the situation.

> Though the number of the children of Israel be as the sand of the sea, a remnant shall be saved: for he [God] will finish the work, and cut it short in righteousness: because a short work will the Lord make upon the earth (Romans 9:27, 28).

To the church of the last days, the True Witness says, "As many as I love, I rebuke and chasten: be zealous therefore, and repent" (Revelation 3:19).

When Christ will have sifted and purified His church (see Amos 9:9-12), when His character is reproduced in the lives of His people, then the "offense of the cross" will again become a reality, and history will repeat itself. Then the divided world will unite itself against its common enemy, Christ's church. God's people will once again be put to an open shame and suffer affliction and death (see Matthew 24:9, 10; Luke 6:22). At that time, the glory of God must shine through us as we rejoice to be counted worthy to suffer shame for His name (see Acts 5:41). We will take courage from Peter's words, "For even hereunto were ye called: because Christ also suffered for us, leaving us an example, that ye should follow in his steps" (1 Peter 2:21).

The blood of Christ

The second significant thing that occurred at Calvary involves *what God did to His Son on the cross*. It is not enough to simply know the truth of the cross; we must also be touched by its power if it is to be of value to us.

On the cross, God placed the sins of every person upon Christ, our Sin Bearer. The sin of Adam, which brought condemnation to all mankind, plus the sins of everyone born in this world were all heaped on our Substitute (see Isaiah 53:6). God did not spare His own Son, but measured out the full wages of sin upon Him so that "by one offering he [Christ] hath perfected forever them that are sanctified" (Hebrews 10:14; cf. 9:25-28). This supreme sacrifice is the fulfillment of the many sacrifices offered in the sanctuary service of the Old Testament; it is called "the blood of Christ" in the New Testament.

The New Testament writers place infinite value on the blood of Christ. It is able to redeem us (see 1 Peter 1:18, 19), justify us (see Romans 5:9), cleanse us from all sins (1 John 1:7), cancel the guilt of our many sins (see Matthew 26:27, 28), and make peace between sinful humans and a holy God (see Colossians 1:20). These are but some of the attributes the New Testament ascribes to the precious blood of Christ.

Before we can discover the power of Christ's blood in the life of the believer, we need to understand the significance of this expression, "the blood of Christ."

In Scripture, Christ's blood plays a vital role when it comes to dealing with sin. "Almost all things are by the law purged with blood; and without the shedding of blood is no remission" (Hebrews 9:22). This is because shed blood indicates that life has been laid down in death. God said, "The life of the flesh is in the blood: and I have given it to you upon the altar to make an atonement for your souls: for it is the blood that maketh an atonement for the soul" (Leviticus 17:11).

All the blood shed in the different sacrifices of the Old Testament was a representation of the blood of Christ—that is to say, of His life, which He laid down on the cross for the sins of the world. We must never interpret the expression "the blood of Christ" to refer to His literal human blood. This was no different from our blood (see Hebrews 2:14) and had no saving power in and of itself. "The blood of Christ" signifies His divine life—original, unborrowed, underived—that He gave up in exchange for our condemned life. It was our condemned life that died eternally in Him. This is the supreme sacrifice that saves us from the guilt and punishment of sin, that qualifies us to live. This is what the power of the blood is all about.

According to Scripture, Christ's blood saves us in three ways: in relation to God, in relation to humanity, and in relation to Satan.

In relation to God. As well as being the transgression of the law, sin "is of the devil" (1 John 3:8). Therefore, our sins have a marked effect upon our relationship with God. "Your iniquities have separated between you and your God, and your sins have hid his face from you, that he will not hear" (Isaiah 59:2). Sin separates us from God and fractures our relationship with Him.

Of course, this puts us in a hopeless situation because He is the source of all life; we cannot live apart from Him. How, then, can sinful human beings be reconciled to a holy God? The only answer is the blood of Christ. "When we were enemies, we were reconciled to God by the death [blood, verse 9] of his Son" (Romans 5:10). When, by faith, the blood of Christ is applied to our lives of sin, reconciliation takes place between us and God. "Therefore being justified by faith, we have peace with God through our Lord Jesus Christ" (Romans 5:1; cf. John 14:27).

Not only does the blood of Christ reconcile us to God when we first come to Him in faith, but more than this, it continues to cleanse and forgive us daily as we abide in Him, confessing our sins (see 1 John 1:7, 9). The power of Christ's blood never loses its efficacy to save us from our sins. Thus, our relationship with God is never broken; we can come to Him boldly every time through the blood of Christ no matter what our experience may have been (see Hebrews 10:19-22).

Many of us find our prayer life hindered because we insist on looking at ourselves and our failures rather than coming to God in the merits of Christ's blood. No matter what our Christian experience may be, we must approach God only by the blood of His Son. And through that blood we may always come boldly, without shame or fear.

In relation to humanity. Sin brings guilt and stress to our human relationships as well as disrupting our relationship with God. All of us are familiar with guilt. Guilt is unpleasant; in fact, medical science confirms that the great majority of human sickness and woe can be traced to the problem of guilt. The devil and the world offer many remedies to guilt, but none can truly or permanently save us from the pain. Only the blood of Christ can rescue us from the guilty conscience (see Hebrews 9:14; 10:2).

A person who has been touched by the power of Christ's blood is among the happiest people in the world, no matter what else he may have to put up with in this life. Not only does he have peace with God through the blood of Christ, but he has also found inner peace with himself through this same blood. David, who knew something of God's power to forgive, said, "Blessed [happy] is the man unto whom the Lord imputeth not iniquity, and in whose spirit there is no guile" (Psalm 32:2). This same privilege belongs to every believer whose faith rests in the blood of Christ.

In relation to Satan. Our sins produce a third effect. They give Satan, the enemy of our souls, opportunity to accuse us before God. Revelation 12:10 tells us that Satan accuses Christians before God night and day. And his accusations are true, for we have committed many sins that neither we nor God can deny. How can we meet these accusations? Verse 11 of Revelation 12 gives us the answer: "They overcame him [Satan and his accusations] by the blood of the Lamb." The blood of Christ is able to meet every accusation Satan makes against us.

On the basis of His blood, Christ our advocate and mediator rebukes every accusation of the devil (see Zechariah 3:1-4; Jude 9). The cause of Satan's defeat every time is the wonderful power of the blood of Christ. "Who is he that condemneth?" asks Paul. "It is Christ that died, yea rather, that is risen again, who is even at the right hand of God, who also maketh intercession for us" (Romans 8:34).

In the Jewish calendar, the Day of Atonement stood out as more important than any other day of the year, for it pointed to final judgment. On this day, the true people of God were cleansed from all their sins (see Leviticus 16:30). How was this realized? By the blood of the Lord's goat (see Leviticus 16:9, 15, 16), which symbolized Christ's blood (see Hebrews 9:11, 12). The hope of every believer in the day of judgment, therefore, is not his or her personal goodness, but the blood of Christ and His righteousness.

> Herein is our love made perfect, that we may have boldness in the day of judgment: because as he [Christ] is, so are we in this world (1 John 4:17).

Satan does not confine his accusations of us to God. He also enjoys pointing his finger at us and bringing home his accusations to our own hearts. Each time we fall into sin or fail to meet God's ideal, Satan immediately takes advantage and tries to discourage us by accusing us through our consciences. How do we react to such accusations? Do we fall under them, feel defeated, and give up? Or do we respond, "Yes, I am a sinner, and I have sinned terribly. But I have found mercy"? If we would be free of Satan's accusations and the burden of our guilt, there is power in the blood of Christ. All that is required is that we avail ourselves of it by faith.

This, then, is what is involved in the wonderful power of Christ's blood, made available to us through God's "unspeakable gift" (2 Corinthians 9:15). By it, we are reconciled to God. By it, our guilty consciences are purged so that we have an inner peace that passes understanding (see Philippians 4:7). And by it, we are able to meet any accusation of the devil. No wonder the New Testament writers place such infinite value on the blood of Christ. And we must do the same.

The cross of Christ
Now we must turn our attention to the third application of the truth of Christ's cross: *What God did for the human race in Christ on the cross.* As we have already seen, the whole human race died "in Christ" at the cross.

Why did God include all of humanity in the death of His Son? Was it not enough that Christ bore the sins of the whole world?

Scripture gives two main reasons why it was necessary for God to include the whole human race in the death of His Son. First, it was necessary in order that we might be legally delivered from our condemned status "in Adam" (see Romans 5:12-21). "For as in Adam all die, even so in Christ shall all be made alive" (1 Corinthians 15:22).

Second, it was necessary for God to include all mankind in Christ's death because it was the only way He could free us from the power of sin (see Romans 6:7). To understand this, we have to understand the dual nature of sin. Sin is not only an *act* of transgressing the law that makes us guilty before God and brings us under the condemnation of the law. It is also a *power* that has us in its grip. Paul makes this clear in Romans 7:14-24, where he describes the typical situation of someone who wants to do good but finds that he is unable to do so because he is captive to the law of sin. No matter how much we may determine in and of ourselves to follow righteousness, the principle of sin that dominates our lives makes this impossible. "That which is born of flesh is flesh," Jesus told Nicodemus (John 3:6). He meant that human nature cannot change itself. The Bible clearly teaches that our human nature, the natural life we inherit from Adam, is unable to keep the law or to do righteousness; it is naturally at enmity against God (see Romans 8:7).

It is a wonderful fact that Christ died for our sins on the cross so that we might be forgiven. But you have discovered, I'm sure, that forgiveness, as marvelous as it is, is not enough. You want *deliverance* from sin; otherwise, your life is a vicious circle of sinning and being forgiven, then sinning again. At the least, this is frustrating. Sinful acts may be forgiven and blotted out through the blood of Christ, but our basic sinful natures cannot be merely forgiven; they must be destroyed. For example, God can forgive me for losing my temper or for acting selfishly, but He cannot forgive my disposition to lose my temper or my basic selfishness. These must be ended, or to be more specific, they must be crucified. That is why God included you and me in the death that took place on Christ's cross.

The great mistake most people make when they first come to Christ is to think that their natural life of sin can be changed or reformed so that it will be made pleasing to God. As a result, most

Christians begin their Christian life by making promises to God. Sooner or later, depending on how strong the willpower is, we all discover that such promises are like ropes of sand. No matter how hard we try, the result is always the same—failure.

What is the problem?

We have failed to see that the sinful life of the flesh is beyond repair. We have to recognize that our sinful human nature cannot be rebuilt into something that will be acceptable to God. That is why He included us in the death of His Son on the cross. We were crucified "in Christ," and in exchange He has given us the very life of Jesus to replace, not repair, our sinful human nature. Unlike every other world religion, Christianity offers mankind, not a changed life, but an exchanged life. The sooner we realize that perfecting the flesh is impossible (see Galatians 3:1-3), the sooner we will surrender to the formula of the gospel: "I am crucified with Christ: nevertheless I live; yet not I, but Christ liveth in me" (Galatians 2:20).

The greatest discovery an unbeliever can make is that Christ died for him. But the greatest discovery a believer can make is that he has been crucified with Christ and that now his life is hid in Christ (see Colossians 3:3). Such a discovery will bring to an end all self-effort in our lives. Instead, we will "live by the faith of the Son of God, who loved me, and gave himself for me" (Galatians 2:20).

Conclusion

The blood of Christ, then, is God's solution in dealing with all our sins, but the cross of Christ is His remedy for delivering us from the very source of sin. The first is the means of our justification, while the second is the means of our sanctification. Just as we cannot obtain forgiveness from our sins unless we see Christ bearing *all our sins* on the cross, so we cannot know deliverance from sin's power unless we see Christ bearing *us* on the cross.

Sanctification, victory over sin, involves a dual process. On the one hand, we surrender totally, by faith, to our death in Christ so that, on the other hand, the Spirit of Christ who indwells us may manifest the life of Christ in us and through us. The apostle Paul describes this process in these words:

Always bearing about in the body the dying of the Lord Jesus, that the life also of Jesus might be made manifest in our body. For we which live are alway delivered unto death for Jesus' sake, that the life also of Jesus might be made manifest in our mortal flesh (2 Corinthians 4:10, 11; cf. Philippians 3:10).

When we combine the blood of Christ (His death for our sins) with the cross of Christ (our death in Him), we have indeed discovered the wonderful power of the cross. That cross and its power "is to them that perish foolishness; but unto us that are saved it is the power of God" (1 Corinthians 1:18).

Key Points in Chapter 13
The Principle of the Cross

1. When Christ was crucified, three things took place that vitally affect the life of every believer:
   a. What Satan and the world did to Christ on the cross;
   b. what God did to His Son on the cross;
   c. what God did for the human race in Christ on the cross.

2. Satan and the world showed their utter hatred for Christ on the cross, putting Him to an open shame. When we take Christ's cross as our own, Satan and the world will likewise manifest their hatred toward us. The Bible calls this "the offense of the cross" (Galatians 5:11).

3. God placed the sins of every person upon Christ, our Sin Bearer, as He hung on the cross. The New Testament refers to this as "the blood of Christ" (see 1 Peter 1:18, 19; Romans 5:9; 1 John 1:7).
   a. The "blood" of Christ, as used in the New Testament, does not refer to His literal, human blood. It refers to His supreme sacrifice—His divine life, which He gave up in exchange for our condemned life.
   b. The "blood" of Christ reconciles sinful human beings to a holy God.
   c. The "blood" of Christ rescues us from a guilty conscience.
   d. On the basis of His "blood," Christ is able to rebuke every accusation of the devil against us.

4. God included all of humanity in the death of His Son in order to free us from the power of sin.
   a. Sin is not only an act of transgression that makes us guilty; it is also a power that has us in its grip.
   b. Forgiveness, marvelous as it is, is not enough. We must have deliverance from sin.
   c. Sinful acts may be forgiven and blotted out by the blood of Christ, but our basic, sinful natures cannot be merely forgiven—they must be destroyed or crucified (see Galatians 5:24).

5. The sinful human nature is beyond repair; it cannot be rebuilt into something acceptable to God. That is why God included us in the death of His Son. We were crucified "in Christ," and in exchange God gives us the very life of Jesus to replace, not repair, our sinful human nature.

Chapter Fourteen

The Work
of the Holy Spirit

As we have seen repeatedly in this book so far, salvation full and complete has already been prepared and provided for us in Christ Jesus. This is the objective gospel. The Holy Spirit's work is to communicate this completed salvation to the fallen human race. His role, then, in our *experience* of salvation is vital.

At the end of His earthly ministry, Jesus told His disciples that after He returned to heaven the Father would send the Holy Spirit to be with them. The Spirit would guide them into all truth and make real in their experience the salvation Christ had prepared for them (see John 16:13-15; 2 Corinthians 3:17, 18). We need to understand the work of the Spirit in our salvation so that we will know how to cooperate with Him. The Holy Spirit's work is threefold. It has to do with the life of (1) the unbeliever; (2) the believer; and (3) the church. In this chapter and the next, we will look at each in turn.

The Spirit's work
in the life of the unbeliever

No matter how educated or intelligent a person may be, the truth of the gospel is beyond the reach of his or her natural mind. The natural intellect cannot discover the gospel (see Matthew 16:16, 17; 1 Corinthians 2:10-14; 12:3). Further, the gospel is actually foolishness to our human way of thinking (see 1 Corinthians 1:18). Thus without the Holy Spirit, no one could discern the truth as it is in Christ or be convicted of it, no matter how familiar he or she might be with the Scriptures. Spiritual things are spiritually discerned (see 1 Corinthians 2:10-14). Human beings simply cannot experience the power of the gospel without the enabling of the Holy Spirit. (Incidentally, this is why no Christian can claim that he has "won" a soul to Christ; this privilege belongs solely to the Holy Spirit. At our best, we can be only instruments in the hands of God through which the gospel is witnessed.)

Jesus clearly indicates what the work of the Holy Spirit is to be in regard to the world. "When he [the Holy Spirit] is come, he will reprove the world [unbelievers] of sin, and of righteousness, and of judgment" (John 16:8). This is the first step in salvation. Sinful, fallen human beings must be convicted of sin, of righteousness, and of judgment. It is the work of the Holy Spirit to do this through the preaching of the gospel.

When Jesus said that the Spirit would convict the world "of sin," He did not mean sin in the sense of an act of transgression against the law. He was referring to sin as "unbelief." Verse 9 makes this plain: "Of sin, because they believe not on me" (see also Romans 14:23). Sinful man is not lost because he has committed sins, but because he is without Christ—that is to say, because he is born of Adam and therefore already stands condemned in him even before he commits sins of his own. In an earlier chapter we saw how our eternal destiny does not rest on what we do (our behavior) but on which humanity we belong to. Those who are "in Adam" come under the condemnation of the law, since they are regarded as sinners, while those who are "in Christ" are considered to be righteous and have passed from death into life (see John 5:24). Therefore, the first work of the Holy Spirit in the life of an unbeliever is to convict him that he is a lost sinner because he is not "in Christ" by faith.

Second, the Holy Spirit convicts the unbeliever that righteousness can be found only in Christ. All the righteousness we can produce in and of ourselves is nothing more than filthy rags in God's sight (see Isaiah 64:6). In His explanation of the Spirit's work for the unbeliever, Jesus says the Spirit convicts "of righteousness, because I go to my Father" (John 16:10). By this, He means that the work of redemption, which the Father sent Him to accomplish (see Galatians 4:4, 5), is a finished work. Jesus returned to heaven and the Father because He had completed His redemptive work.

> This man [Christ], after he had offered one sacrifice for sins for ever [a finished work], sat down on the right hand of God; from henceforth expecting till his enemies be made his footstool (Hebrews 10:12, 13).

The work of the Holy Spirit could not begin in the fullest sense until Christ's sacrifice of atonement was complete. Now that Christ is in heaven, having prepared salvation full and complete by a perfect sacrifice, it is the work of the Holy Spirit to finish the work of atonement in sinful men and women who are willing to believe (see Romans 5:11).

Finally, the Holy Spirit convicts of the judgment "because the prince of this world is judged" (John 16:11). Everyone who hears the gospel must be made aware that this world, which is under Satan's control, has already been judged and sentenced to destruction.

The only hope for those who belong to the world is to respond by faith to the free gift of salvation in Christ (see John 3:16). And there is good news in this judgment. Jesus explains that the judgment of the prince of this world consists in his being "cast out" (John 12:31). The sinner can rejoice to believe that Satan is "cast out" of his life when he exercises faith in the Savior.

The preaching of the everlasting gospel is to be realized anew in the last days (see Matthew 24:14; Revelation 14:6). It includes the fact that "Babylon the great [symbol of Satan's world, including worldly Christianity] is fallen, is fallen, and is become the habitation of devils" (Revelation 18:2). The fires of everlasting destruction have been prepared only for "the devil and his angels" (Matthew 25:41), but if individuals willfully reject the free gift of salvation provided for them in Christ from the foundation of the world (see verse 34), then God has no alternative but to include them in the destruction of this doomed world (see Mark 16:15, 16; John 3:18; Hebrews 10:26-29). Mankind's only hope is to respond to God's plea to "come out of her [Babylon] my people, that ye be

not partakers of her sins, and that ye receive not of her plagues"
(Revelation 18:4).

The experience of conversion

Before we look at the second aspect of the Spirit's work—His
work in the life of the believer—we need to be sure we understand
the mechanics of the conversion experience.

When a person responds positively to the Spirit's threefold
conviction, when he repents, believes, and is baptized (see Mark
1:14, 15; 16:15, 16), a radical change takes place in his life. The
Holy Spirit actually comes and dwells in him (see Acts 2:37-41).
The Bible calls this experience "regeneration," or "the new birth"
(see John 3:3-5; Titus 3:5; 1 Peter 1:23). This indwelling of the
Holy Spirit is the same as receiving the life of Christ (see Romans
8:2, 10); it is this that subjectively changes a person's status from
being "in Adam" to being "in Christ" and qualifies him for heaven
(see Romans 8:9).

Thus we may say that the work of the Holy Spirit in the life of
the *unbeliever* is from without, while the Spirit's work in the life
of the *believer* is from within. Both the unbeliever and the
believer experience the Holy Spirit's convictions regarding truth
in their consciences. But the unbeliever is not "indwelt" by the
Holy Spirit, so that these convictions are coming to him from
outside. The believer, however, has the Holy Spirit dwelling in
him (see 1 Corinthians 3:16; 6:19), so that the Spirit's convictions
are coming to him from within.

This is an important distinction. Jesus made it clear to
Nicodemus that "except a man be born again, he cannot see the
kingdom of God" (John 3:3). As long as a person is not "indwelt" by
the Holy Spirit, he is in a lost state even though he may receive
conviction from the Holy Spirit or may even be a member of the
church (see Romans 8:9). But to be born again of the Holy Spirit
means to be made alive from the death of sin. This new birth was
first realized objectively in Christ at His incarnation when His
divinity was united to our corporate humanity (see Ephesians
2:5), and it is made effective to us by the new-birth experience
through faith (see Acts 2:38). This is genuine conversion, the
beginning of the Christian life.

To be converted is the same thing as being born of the Holy

Spirit, which is the same thing as the new birth. It is this experience that changes our status from an unbeliever to a believer. It is this experience that also subjectively justifies us (see James 5:20) and places us in a position in which sanctification is possible because now we possess the very life of Christ through the indwelling Spirit of Christ (see Romans 8:2, 11-13).

The Spirit's work
in the life of the believer

The work of the Holy Spirit in the life of the believer is to reproduce in him or her the character of Jesus Christ, which is the character of God (see John 14:9).

Human beings were originally created with the Holy Spirit dwelling in them so that they might reflect God's character. But because of Adam's fall, we are born into this world without God, spiritually bankrupt. The purpose of the gospel—besides saving us—is to undo the damage caused by Adam's sin and to restore the divine image in us. The starting point of this process—the gospel as a subjective experience—is the new birth. In other words, the prerequisite for holy living is being born of the Spirit. In the humanity of Christ and through His redeeming work, full provision has already been made for restoring God's image in mankind. But it is the work of the Holy Spirit to make this provision real in the life of every believer who has become one with Christ and who is living by faith.

The first task of the Spirit is to deliver us from our position "in Adam" and establish us "in Christ" and His church. Having done that, the Holy Spirit then dwells in us in order to bring about the deeper work of Christ's cross in which the old life is put to death in reality—more and more so daily—that Christ's life may be increasingly manifested in us (see 2 Corinthians 4:10, 11; 3:17, 18; Ephesians 3:16-19; 4:4-13).

Holy living is not left up to us to produce; it is solely the work of the Holy Spirit living in us. If we truly realized this, self-effort would cease, and we would make room for the Holy Spirit to produce in us the life of Jesus. This does not mean that we have nothing to do. Denying self so that the Holy Spirit may manifest Jesus' life in us requires a constant, unrelenting battle. This is what the Bible calls "the good fight of faith" (1 Timothy 6:12).

The Holy Spirit's work in the life of the believer is nothing less than sanctification. According to the apostle Paul, it involves the spirit, soul, and body (see 1 Thessalonians 5:23).

What does Paul mean by these terms? Just as a doctor needs to know how the human body is put together in order to treat us physically, so believers need to know how we are put together spiritually in order to cooperate with the Holy Spirit in the work of sanctification. Physically, we are made up of various organs, each having a function within the body that is both distinct and yet closely related to the function of every other organ. Spiritually, we are made up of three components—spirit, soul, and body—each of which has a specific work in the spiritual well-being of the whole, but which is also closely related to the other components.

The great error of the Christian church following the apostolic period was to separate the body from the soul and to give the soul a separate existence independent of the body. This idea comes from the religion of the Greeks, not from Scripture. According to the Bible, each of these three spiritual components has a distinct function that contributes to the spiritual existence of the whole man, but none is able to exist independently of the others. At death, the whole person—spirit, soul, and body—dies (see Ezekiel 18:4, 20; Ecclesiastes 9:5, 6; 8:8).

When we examine the spiritual structure of mankind as described in the Bible, we find a significant parallel between that structure and God's temple or sanctuary. In fact, the apostle Paul says, "Know ye not that ye are the temple of God, and that the Spirit of God dwelleth in you?" (1 Corinthians 3:16; cf. 6:19). This is because the Old Testament sanctuary was a symbol of the incarnate Christ (see Psalm 29:9; John 2:19-21; Revelation 21:3; also compare Psalm 77:13 with John 14:4-6). And Christ, in turn, is the prototype of the believer (see Ephesians 2:19-22; 1 Peter 2:5; Hebrews 3:4-6; 1 Corinthians 6:16).

God's promises to us under the new covenant are the reality of the symbols seen in the sanctuary of the old covenant. For example, in the old covenant, the law was written on tables of stone and placed in the ark. In the new covenant, the same law is written on our hearts and placed in the "inward man" (Romans 7:22). In the old covenant, God dwelt in the innermost part of the sanctuary, while in the new covenant, God dwells in the inner-most part of man through His Holy Spirit (see Ezekiel 36:27; John 14:17; Romans 8:9, 11). In the old covenant, the sanctuary structure represented the heavenly temple of God, but in the new covenant, the Christian himself becomes God's temple (see 1 Corinthians 3:16, 17; 6:19).

Thus, just as God formerly dwelt in the tabernacle (see Exodus 25:8), so the Holy Spirit dwells in the believer today. The sanctuary of the old covenant was divided into three parts—the court-yard, the Holy Place, and the Most Holy Place (see Exodus 25:8-27; Hebrews 9:2-4). Likewise, the believer, who represents God's temple on earth, is divided into three parts spiritually—spirit, soul, and body.

The body, with its various members, may be compared to the courtyard of the temple, occupying an external position with its life visible to all. This is the place of sacrifice (see Romans 12:1; Colossians 3:5).

Inside is man's soul, the faculties of his mind—the emotions, will, intellect—through which God operates. This corresponds to the Holy Place, where the priests carried out their daily ministry.

Innermost, behind the second veil and within man's self-consciousness, lies the human spirit, which may be compared to the Most Holy Place of the temple—the dwelling place of God. In the converted individual, the Holy Spirit dwells in his or her spirit; it represents "the secret place of the Most High" (Psalm 91:1).

Please note that the application of the earthly sanctuary to the believer does not in any way deny the real existence of a heavenly sanctuary (see Hebrews 8:1, 2). The Bible clearly teaches that God dwells in heaven as well as in the believer (see Isaiah 57:15).

The sanctuary was a representation of Christ's humanity and also, by extension, of those who believe on Him. As we have seen, in the new covenant, believers are identified as God's temple. In other words, the sanctuary of the Old Testament represented first the incarnate Christ and the believer who is "in Him" (the objective gospel). Second, it also represented the Christian who has Christ living in him or her (the subjective gospel).

Thus we may say that the Old Testament sanctuary was God's model of the everlasting gospel that was first fulfilled in Christ and that must now be realized in the church, of which each believer is a part. The cleansing of the heavenly sanctuary is a work accomplished by Christ, our High Priest, but it is contingent on the cleansing of the hearts of His people on earth.

In the next chapter we will consider the place and function of each of these three spiritual components of mankind—spirit, soul, and body—and their relationship to the work of the Holy Spirit.

Key Points in Chapter 14
The Work of the Holy Spirit

1. The work of the Holy Spirit is to communicate to the fallen human race the completed salvation prepared and provided for us in Christ Jesus.
2. The Holy Spirit's work in the life of the *unbeliever* may be summarized as follows (see John 16:8):
   a. First, He convicts the unbeliever that he is a lost sinner because he is not "in Christ" by faith.
   b. Second, He convicts the unbeliever that salvation can be found only in Christ.
   c. Third, He convicts the unbeliever of judgment—that this world, under Satan's control, has already been judged and sentenced to destruction.
3. When an unbeliever responds to the Holy Spirit, a radical change takes place in his life. The Holy Spirit actually comes and dwells in him (see Acts 2:37-41). This is the same as the "new birth," or conversion. It changes a person's status from being "in Adam" to being "in Christ" (see Romans 8:9).
4. The Holy Spirit's work in the life of the *believer* is to dwell in him so that the old life is put to death in reality—more and more so daily—that Christ's life may be increasingly manifested (see 2 Corinthians 4:10, 11; 3:17, 18; Ephesians 3:16-19; 4:4-13). This is sanctification.
5. Spiritually, we are made up of three components: body, soul, and spirit. There is a significant parallel between this spiritual structure of mankind and God's temple or sanctuary. Just as God dwelt in the sanctuary, the Holy Spirit lives in the believer today (see 1 Corinthians 3:16).
   a. The body corresponds to the courtyard of the sanctuary.
   b. The soul (the faculties of the mind, will, and emotions) corresponds to the Holy Place of the sanctuary.
   c. The spirit (the human self-consciousness) corresponds to the Most Holy Place of the sanctuary.

Chapter Fifteen

Spirit, Soul, and Body

In the previous chapter, we saw that spiritually we are made up of three components—spirit, soul, and body. Each of these has a specific work in the spiritual well-being of the whole, but each is also closely related to the others. In this chapter, we will look at each of these components and their relationship to the Holy Spirit's work in our lives. Then we will examine the Spirit's work in the life of the church.

The first component—the spirit

The following texts clearly teach that each of us, as created by God, possesses a spirit:

> Saith the Lord, which . . . formeth the spirit of man within him (Zechariah 12:1).
> For what man knoweth the things of a man, save the spirit of man which is in him? (1 Corinthians 2:11).
> The Spirit itself beareth witness with our spirit that we are the children of God (Romans 8:16).

God is a spirit (see John 4:24), so when He said, "Let us make man in our image, after our likeness" (Genesis 1:26), it was primarily this aspect of our being—our spirit—that He had in mind. This spirit is not our breath, our soul, or the Holy Spirit. It is the component in us that above all else distinguishes us from the animals and makes us spiritual beings accountable to God. It is because human beings have a spirit that we find even the most primitive people worshiping in some form. The human spirit wants to commune with the spiritual world just as our bodies interact with the physical world and our minds (souls) interact with other minds. We are spiritual, physical, and social beings because we are made up of spirit, body, and soul.

God formed in us this spiritual component in order that it might be His point of contact with us—His dwelling place in us. Through our spirits, He would direct our minds (our souls), which in turn would control our bodies (see Colossians 2:19). Thus the entire person, living in total dependence on God, would reflect His character of selfless love (see 1 John 4:7, 8). This was God's original plan for us when He created our first parents.

Sad to say, sin marred God's plan. When Adam and Eve sinned, the Holy Spirit left them, leaving their spirits vacant for Satan to occupy. Selfishness replaced unselfish love, and their lives were darkened spiritually (see 2 Peter 2:19). This is the nature with which all their children have been born; we come into the world without the indwelling Spirit of God, slaves to the devil and sin. Everyone is born into this world uninhabited by God's Spirit and can therefore walk only "according to the course of this world, according to the prince of the power of the air, the spirit that now worketh in the children of disobedience" (Ephesians 2:2).

But we have not been left without hope. The plan of redemption, formulated in God's mind "before the foundation of the world" (Ephesians 1:4), was designed to recover us fully from our fallen state and restore in us the image of God. In His humanity, Christ prepared this restoration for each of us, and the work of the Holy Spirit now makes it available to us.

Before conversion, our spirit is not indwelt by God's Spirit. Except for the conviction the Holy Spirit brings to us from without, we can hardly feel our spirit's function in the life. Therefore, prior to the new birth, we are dominated by the soul, or mind, and its preoccupation with self—or by the body with its lusts. At conversion, our spirit is made alive because the Holy Spirit comes and dwells in us. Our spirit becomes God's dwelling place and the seat of His will in our lives. This is the new-birth experience that is absolutely essential to justification and that is the prerequisite to sanctification, the process by which God's character is reproduced in us.

When we experience the new birth, we receive the life of Christ in the person of the Holy Spirit. Scripture describes such a person as a babe in Christ (see 1 Corinthians 3:1). We are saved from the guilt and punishment of sin; we are accounted righteous, but we still have to learn to "walk in the Spirit" (Galatians 5:16) just as a newborn baby has to learn to walk on its feet.

Two things will be manifested as the Holy Spirit increases in strength in our lives. First, our characters will begin to reflect more and more the character of Christ. Second, we will begin to be able to distinguish between that which proceeds from our spirit and that which comes from the self-life of the soul. Hebrews 4:12 speaks of this as the separation between soul and spirit that the Word produces.

God regenerates us, teaches us, and leads us into His rest through our spirits. But sad to say, because of long years of bondage to the self-life of the soul, many of us know very little of the "Spirit of life" that dwells in us and is able to make us "free from the law of sin and death" (Romans 8:2). We need to earnestly ask God daily to teach us what is spiritual and what proceeds merely from the emotions of the soul. Even in our Bible study, we tend to rely more on our mental ability than on letting the Spirit guide us into all truth (see 1 Corinthians 2:12-14; John 16:13).

The second component—the soul

The soul is the component that makes us human. It includes the ability to think and learn and choose, our ideals, love, hate, feelings, discernment, etc. The seat and essence of our personality is found in the soul; here is where we find the faculties of the mind (see Job 7:15), the will (see Proverbs 2:10, 19), knowledge (see 2 Samuel 5:8; Job 10:1; John 12:27), and the emotions. For this reason, we often find both the Old and New Testaments using the word *soul* to refer simply to a human being, a person (see Genesis 14:21; Exodus 1:5; Deuteronomy 10:22; Acts 2:41; 7:14; Romans 13:1).

Since the soul is the seat of our personalities, it is the seat of the real "I." That is why Scripture often uses the word *soul* as a personal pronoun, i.e., *I, you, me* (see Genesis 12:13; Deuteronomy 23:24; Mark 14:34). Our soul, then, is simply our *self* (see Leviticus 11:43; Esther 9:31). Thus everything that originates from the soul is polluted with self, which the Bible equates with iniquity. That is why the judgment condemns self-righteous acts as works of iniquity (Matthew 7:21-23).

The soul, with its life of self, is our natural life. The Bible also calls this "the flesh" (see Galatians 3:3; Romans 8:4). We inherit this life at birth; it is the only life the unconverted person can live. Nothing we can do of ourselves can change this life—not even education or culture. This is also the life of the carnal believer— the one who professes Christ, but who lives in contradiction to Christ and the life of the Holy Spirit.

In the one who is sanctified, however, the self-life of the soul is crucified through the cross of Christ (see Galatians 5:24). That which proceeds from the soul (the mind) and also the behavior of the body is now under the direction of the Holy Spirit as He dwells in the believer's spirit. Such a life is actually the life of Christ reproduced in the believer.

This brings us to the main point—the Holy Spirit's work in the life of the believer. The Holy Spirit dwells in the believer's spirit, but it is in the soul, or mind, that He operates. In the Old Testament sanctuary, God dwelt in the Most Holy Place (representing our spirits) but directed His people through the ministry of the Holy Place (representing our soul or mind). The same parallel exists in the human temple. God's Spirit dwells in our spirits, but He operates through our souls or minds. Philippians 2:5 calls this having the mind of Christ.

Our bodies, and therefore our behavior, are never directly controlled by the Holy Spirit. He controls our bodies through our souls, or minds. Again the parallel exists in the Old Testament sanctuary. It was impossible for God to communicate from the Most Holy Place (our spirits) to the courtyard (our bodies) except through the Holy Place (our souls).

To see how this actually works, we need to look at the life of Christ, for He is our prototype and example. His humanity was identical in every point to ours (see Hebrews 2:17), so the body He received through Mary was a body of sin (see Galatians 4:4; Romans 1:3) dominated by the law of sin (see Romans 8:2, 3).

This is how He could be (and was) tempted in all points as we are (see Hebrews 4:15).

However, Christ was also born of the Spirit from His very conception (see Luke 1:35). So from the very beginning of His life on earth, Christ's mind, or soul, was under the full control of the Holy Spirit, who dwelt in His human spirit. "The child grew, and waxed strong in spirit" (Luke 2:40; cf. Luke 4:1).

Christ's temptations came to Him the same way ours come to us—through the sinful (selfish) desires of the flesh. It was through bodily wants that Satan tempted Him in the wilderness to use His divine power to satisfy self, independently of His Father's will (see Luke 4:2-4). It was His natural fear of death (self-love of the flesh) that led Jesus three times to plead with His Father to remove the bitter cup of the cross (see Mark 14:34-41).

But the self-centered desires of the flesh cannot be satisfied without the consent of the mind. Temptation, in and of itself, does not become sin until the mind *consents* to the temptation. "When lust hath conceived [in the mind], it bringeth forth sin" (James 1:15). Since Christ's mind was under the full control of the Holy Spirit, His response to every temptation was "No!" "Not my will [self], but thine [God's] be done" (Luke 22:42). Therefore, sin had no part in His life (see John 6:38). Instead, He condemned sin (the law of sin) in the flesh (see Romans 8:2, 3).

Christ's flesh, being our corporate sinful flesh, lusted after sin. But His mind, being spiritual, never yielded to sin, and thus He conquered sin in the flesh through the power of the Spirit (see Luke 4:13, 14). Likewise, if we have the mind of Christ, if we put on the Lord Jesus Christ, we will make no "provision for the flesh, to fulfill the lust thereof" (Romans 13:14).

Hebrews 2:18 reads, "In that he [Christ] himself hath suffered being tempted, he is able to succour them that are tempted." Every time Christ was tempted, He suffered. We know that Christ was tempted as we are; otherwise, His being able "to succour them that are tempted" would be meaningless. But the question we must ask is: *Where* did Christ suffer being tempted? The answer is found in 1 Peter 4:1. "Forasmuch then as Christ hath suffered for us *in the flesh*, arm yourselves likewise with the same mind: for he that hath suffered in the flesh hath ceased from sin" (emphasis supplied). Please note that the suffering Peter is talking about here has to do with Christ's victory over sin; it is *not* limited to His suffering on the cross. Being tempted in the flesh, Christ suffered in the flesh (see Hebrews 2:10), but His victory was in the mind. So also, says Peter, if we arm ourselves with the mind of Christ (the mind of the Spirit), sin will cease in our lives, but the flesh will suffer. This, as we will see later in this chapter, is because the nature of the flesh cannot change; it will always desire to sin and must therefore suffer if not satisfied.

So it is in the mind, or the soul, that Christ gives us victory over sin through His indwelling Spirit. As Paul said, "With the mind I myself serve the law of God; but with the flesh the law of sin" (Romans 7:25). Also, he tells us, "Be not conformed to this world: but be ye transformed by the renewing of your mind, that ye may prove what is that good, and acceptable, and perfect, will of God" (Romans 12:2).

In the unbeliever, perfect harmony exists between the soul (the mind) and the body; both are equally under the dominion of sin. Paul reminded the Ephesian Christians of their life before conversion, which was "fulfilling the desires of the flesh and of the mind" (Ephesians 2:3). In the unconverted person, the life of the soul is also the life of the body. Both are contaminated through and through with self.

In the carnal believer, who is born of the Spirit but is still walking after the flesh (the life of self), the mind may desire to do God's will, but the body remains subject to the law of sin (see Romans 7:22, 23). Unaided by the Holy Spirit, the mind cannot overcome the law of sin in our members. Such a life is therefore also marred by sin, although the sins may not be as grievous as those in the life of the unbeliever.

But the spiritual Christian is not only born of the Spirit, he or she is also by faith absolutely surrendered to the Spirit. Such a person has the mind of Christ, so that "the old man" no longer lives in him; Christ lives in him through His Spirit. Thus, "the righteousness of the law might be fulfilled in us, who walk not after the flesh, but after the Spirit" (Romans 8:4).

The third component—the body

As created by God, the body was to be the servant of the soul. The soul, in turn, was to be under the direction of God's Spirit dwelling in man's spirit. Thus the desires of the body, such as sex, hunger, love, etc., would be controlled by God through man's soul; man's behavior would reflect God's character.

When man sinned, he separated himself from God's authority and became independent. The natural desires of the body, now polluted with self, became lust; their purpose became self-satisfaction rather than pleasing God. Man's nature was perverted so that the lust of the flesh became the controlling factor in his life. The life of fallen man came into harmony with the principle of self originated by Satan.

Scripture refers to our bodies in their sinful condition as "the body of sin" (Romans 6:6). This is not because the body is sinful in and of itself, but because the principle of sin has permeated its every member (see Romans 7:23). The self-life that motivates the body is sinful and makes our flesh sinful. And this life of sin is beyond repair. That is why we look forward to the second coming, when our sinful bodies will be redeemed (see Romans 8:23; Philippians 3:20, 21; 1 Corinthians 15:50-54). Until then, the principle of the cross, the principle of self-denial, must daily be applied to our sinful lives through the Holy Spirit (see Luke 9:23).

Sinful human beings are under the power of self, both body and soul, so that even at their very best they are totally self-seeking without God. "All we like sheep have gone astray; we have turned every one to his own way" (Isaiah 53:6; cf. Philippians 2:21; 2 Timothy 3:1, 2). The natural life of mankind is the life of the flesh, made up of the self-life of the soul and body. It is the life we receive at birth (see John 3:6), and we cannot live any other apart from God. We may educate ourselves and become highly cultured, but without the Holy Spirit, we will still live the life of the flesh. Selfishness, in one way or another, will be the controlling factor of our lives. The unconverted person is powerless to fulfill any of God's will because he is "weak through the flesh" (Romans 8:3).

In fact, the flesh is hostile to God and will not, cannot, truly submit to His law (see Galatians 5:17; Romans 8:7). We need to realize that the corruption of the flesh is beyond repair (see 1 Corinthians 15:50-53). Even God Himself, great as His power is, will not transform the flesh into something that is pleasing to Him. The flesh belongs to the realm of Satan, and God has condemned all that belongs to that realm to destruction. This is why Christ crucified the flesh at the cross (see Hebrews 10:19, 20).

Unbelievers, and also many Christians who do not understand God's Word, are always trying to reform or improve the flesh. The flesh can appear good on the surface (it is deceitful, after all, because it is sinful), but within it is "full of hypocrisy and iniquity" (Matthew 23:28). All attempts to improve the flesh, either by punishing the body or by making promises and resolutions, are bound to fail.

"That which is born of the flesh is flesh," Jesus said (John 3:6), and it will always remain so. God Himself recognizes the impossibility of changing the flesh because its originator, the devil, cannot change. So in saving us, God doesn't try to change the flesh. Instead, He has put it to death through the cross and gives us a new life, the life of His Spirit. The flesh must be crucified in order to realize salvation from the power of sin (Galatians 5:24)!

The behavior of the flesh can be manifested in two different ways. The first is sinful acts, which proceed from the desires of the body; you will find a list of these in Galatians 5:19-21 referred to as "the works of the flesh." The second is self-righteous acts, which proceed from the soul. Outwardly, these appear quite different from the works of the flesh; they are commendable, often religious, acts. The self-righteous acts of Paul before his conversion are a good example (see Philippians 3:4-6).

From our human point of view, we highly value self-righteous acts. But God condemns both of these manifestations of the flesh as iniquity (see Isaiah 64:6; Matthew 7:22, 23). The desires of the body make self the center and elevate self-will above God's will. The soul may serve God, but only according to its will—not God's. It may even try with all its might to keep God's law, yet self never fails to be at the heart of every activity. In 1 Corinthians 3:1-3, the apostle Paul divides all believers into two classes: (1) spiritual Christians in whom the indwelling Spirit of God controls the whole person—spirit, soul and body; and (2) carnal Christians who have experienced the new birth (see verse 16), but who are still dominated by the life of the flesh.

The major problem facing the Christian church today is the problem of carnality. Churches are filled with babies in Christ, even though the believers are "old" Christians. This was the problem in the Corinthian and Galatian churches of New Testament times, and it is still the problem of the church today. Every believer needs to learn that there can be no partnership between the flesh and the Spirit, that the only formula for the Christian life is "Not I, but Christ."

Victory over the flesh should be our deep longing in these last days. And this victory is gained through the deeper work of the cross as the Holy Spirit daily brings it to bear upon us. Once we have reckoned ourselves crucified with Christ (see Romans 6:11), we must allow God's Spirit to put this crucifixion into effect, putting to death daily the self of the flesh. Each time self raises its ugly head, the Spirit will bring conviction. Our reaction must be—not to defend or excuse self—but to surrender self to the cross of Christ. When self is completely crucified in us, then the splendor of God's glory will shine forth through our mortal bodies (see Romans 8:11-14). We will then be ready to meet the Lord without dying.

The deeper work of the cross is to crucify self so that the Spirit may reproduce in us the character of Christ. The Bible often speaks of this process as fiery trials and chastenings (see Hebrews 12:5-11; 1 Peter 4:12, 13). Though painful to the flesh at the time, "nevertheless, afterward it yieldeth the peaceable fruit of righteousness to them which are exercised thereby" (Hebrews 12:11). Even for Christ, it was only through suffering in the flesh that He was able to produce righteousness in sinful flesh (see Hebrews 2:10, 18; 5:8, 9). "He that hath suffered in the flesh hath ceased from sin" (1 Peter 4:1).

In examining the work of the Holy Spirit in the life of the believer, it is clear that no aspect of the Christian life is independent of the Spirit's influence. God intends our total lives to be guided and controlled by His Spirit (see Proverbs 3:5, 6). The Holy Spirit is the One who liberates us from the self-life of sin (see 2 Corinthians 3:17, 19); is the means of our sanctification (see 2 Thessalonians 2:13; 1 Peter 1:2); guides us into all truth (see John 16:13); makes our prayers meaningful (see Romans 8:26; Jude 20); and gives us the power to witness to the gospel (see Luke 24:49; Acts 1:8). This is His work in the life of every believer.

The Spirit's work in the life of the church

The Holy Spirit's work doesn't stop with the individual believer; it also involves the life of the whole church. The indwelling

Spirit becomes the link that unites all believers together to form the body of Christ—the church. "By one Spirit are we all baptized into one body, whether we be Jews or Gentiles, whether we be bond or free, and have been all made to drink into one Spirit" (1 Corinthians 12:13). The new birth not only puts us into Christ, it also identifies us with His body so that "we, being many, are one body in Christ, and every one members of one another" (Romans 12:5; cf. 1 Corinthians 10:17; 12:12).

According to the New Testament, the church is a closely knit body of believers with no distinctions whatsoever of race, color, sex, or status (see Galatians 3:26-28). It is a fellowship of men and women who are all one in Christ, by faith, and who are to be perfectly united for the purpose of manifesting the life of God in the same way that Christ manifested it in His human body when He was on earth (see John 14:9; 1 Timothy 3:16).

Sad to say, the Christian church has miserably failed to do this; the world has not really had an opportunity to see, in the church, what God is like. We must realize that salvation in Christ is more than just a personal way to escape eternal damnation. Every person saved in Christ is saved "unto good works" (Ephesians 2:10; cf. Matthew 5:16; Colossians 1:10; 1 Peter 2:12). And these good works are to be carried out in the framework of the church, which is to be as salt and light in the world. Until we who call ourselves Christians are willing to be instruments in the hands of God's Spirit, the world that is more than 75 percent non-Christian will never really witness the power of the gospel.

The apostle Paul makes it clear that every member of the church has a specific function in relationship to the body, as allotted by the Holy Spirit (see Romans 12:5-8; 1 Corinthians 12:14-26; Ephesians 4:11-15). These texts indicate that every believer has been endowed with one or more gifts of the Spirit. These gifts are to be used to minister to the church itself, and they are also the means by which the church, as Christ's representative, is to witness of Him to the world. The church, as Christ's body, is to manifest God in the flesh.

No individual member can fully display Christ completely for the simple reason that no individual member is the total body of Christ. Only through the church as a whole, living in perfect coordination and conformity to the direction of the Holy Spirit, can the life of Christ be fully displayed. This will take place before Christ comes. The Bible calls this "the mystery of God" that will be finished "as he hath declared to his servants the prophets" (Revelation 10:7; cf. Colossians 1:25-27).

Obviously, then, the Holy Spirit has an important work to do in the church as well as in the life of the individual believer. First, the Holy Spirit bestows gifts on the church for the purpose of developing the body of Christ until it grows "unto the measure of the stature of the fullness of Christ" (Ephesians 4:13). Second, the Spirit bestows gifts on the church in order that it may demonstrate and witness to the power of God to a lost world.

Sadly, after almost two thousand years, the church has neither grown into the fullness of Christ, nor has it fully displayed the life of God in the flesh. Should we not, here in the twentieth century, come to God in humility and repentance for our failure? After all, the fault does not lie with God, but with us. It is we who have distorted the truth of the gospel and have put self above the cause of Christ.

Speaking of the last days, Joel proclaimed, "It shall come to pass afterward, that I will pour out my spirit upon all flesh" (Joel 2:28). He goes on to say,

> Therefore also now, saith the Lord, turn ye even to me with all your heart, and with fasting, and with weeping, and with mourning, and rend your heart, and not your garments, and turn unto the Lord your God.... Let the priests, the ministers of the Lord, weep between the porch and the altar, and let them say, Spare thy people, O Lord, and give not thine heritage to reproach, that the heathen should rule over them. Wherefore should they say among the people, Where is their God? Then will the Lord be jealous for his land, and pity his people (Joel 2:12, 13, 17, 18).

This is the deep, heartfelt repentance that God is patiently waiting to hear from His people. "As many as I love, I rebuke and chasten: be zealous therefore, and repent" (Revelation 3:19). When the church realizes this, then God will pour out His Spirit, and the earth will be "lightened with his glory" (Revelation 18:1).

Key Points in Chapter 15
Spirit, Soul, and Body

1. God intended for the spiritual component in mankind—our spirits—to be His point of contact with us, His dwelling place in us. Through our spirits, He intended to direct our souls (our minds), which in turn would control our bodies.

2. Because of Adam's sin, we are all born without the Holy Spirit dwelling in us—slaves to Satan and sin. This is our nature before conversion. When we experience the new birth, we receive the life of Christ in the person of the Holy Spirit, who lives in us.

3. The soul (the mind) is the component in our makeup that enables us to think, learn, choose; it is the area that includes our ideals, love, hate, feelings, and emotions. The Bible often uses the term *soul* to refer simply to a human being (see Genesis 14:21; Exodus 1:5; Acts 2:41; Romans 13:1).

4. The soul, with its life of self, is our natural life. The Bible calls it "the flesh," meaning the human sinful nature.

5. Temptation comes to us (and came to Christ) through the sinful desires of the flesh. But the self-centered desires of the flesh cannot be satisfied without the consent of the mind.

6. Christ's mind, or soul, being spiritual, never yielded to sin; thus He conquered sin in the flesh through the power of the Spirit (see Luke 4:13, 14). Likewise, if we have the mind of Christ, we will make no "provision for the flesh, to fulfill the lusts thereof" (Romans 13:14). It is in the mind, or soul, that Christ gives us victory over sin through His indwelling Spirit.

7. The Bible refers to the third component of our humanity—the body—as "the body of sin" (Romans 6:6). This is not because the body is sinful in and of itself, but because the principle of sin has permeated its members.

8. In saving us, God doesn't try to change the flesh. Instead, He has put it to death through the cross and has given us a new life—the life of His Spirit.

9. The flesh manifests itself in two ways: sinful acts and self-righteous acts. God condemns both as iniquity.

Chapter Sixteen

Law and Grace
I

When I was a missionary in Uganda, a young African approached me one day with a sincere desire to witness for Christ. "Are you saved?" he asked.

After convincing him that I was a Christian, I returned his question. "Are *you* saved?"

"Praise the Lord, I am saved!" he replied enthusiastically.

"If you're saved," I responded, "how is it that I can smell *pombe* [a local beer] on your breath?"

Taken aback, he answered in amazement, "Don't you know that we are saved by grace and not by works?"

So I asked him to explain what he meant.

"Christ did it all," he answered.

"I see," I replied. "You mean He lived a perfect life and died the wages of sin instead of you."

"That's it; you've got it!"

"If that's true," I teased, "then did He also go to heaven instead of you?" Naturally, he was not willing to buy that.

Like this young man, many Christians today fail to understand the biblical meaning of salvation by grace. They accept what the German martyr, Dietrich Bonhoeffer, aptly described as "cheap grace"—the idea that because Christ did it all, Christians have the liberty to live as their sinful natures please. The Bible, of course, teaches no such thing.

How, then, are we to understand this wonderful truth of salvation by grace? Did Christ do away with the law when He saved us by grace?

Tension between law and grace

On the surface, law and grace seem to be antagonistic toward each other. The law demands obedience as a condition of salvation (see Romans 10:5), while grace offers salvation as a free gift without works (see Ephesians 2:8, 9). The law condemns the sinner (see Galatians 3:10), while grace justifies the ungodly (see Romans 4:5). The result is that many who accept God's offer of grace end up rejecting the law. But the Bible—Old Testament and New Testament—does not present grace in opposition to law. Both have their source in God, and God is not self-contradictory.

Many Christians today try to resolve the tension between law and grace through the doctrine of dispensationalism. Dispensationalism divides the Bible into time periods, or dispensations, and teaches that from Moses until Christ, salvation was based on man's obedience to the law under the old covenant. But, says dispensationalism, now that Christ has come and obtained eternal redemption for mankind, salvation comes through the new covenant of grace; the law has been done away with.

This teaching not only denies the unity of Scripture but also contradicts the clear teaching of the New Testament. God has always had only one way of saving sinners, and that is by grace through His redemptive activity in Christ. The apostle Paul says clearly in Romans 4 that Abraham, the father of the Jews, was not saved by circumcision or works or by keeping the law, but by faith in God's promise of salvation in His Son Jesus Christ.

God never gave the law as a means of salvation; that idea is a perversion (see Romans 9:30-33). Paul goes to great lengths to correct this error in his letter to the Galatians (see Galatians 2:16; 5:4). God's main purpose in giving the law was to convict mankind of sin (see Romans 3:20) so that the gift of salvation might become meaningful. "Wherefore the law was our schoolmaster to bring us unto Christ, that we might be justified by faith" (Galatians 3:24).

Because we are self-centered by nature, it doesn't take much to trap us in legalism, which is the attempt to be saved by our obedience to the law. At the heart of every pagan religion is the idea that man must save himself by his own good works. The Bible, however, teaches that this is impossible, that our only hope lies in salvation by faith in God's redeeming grace (see Romans 3:20, 22). "Therefore we conclude that a man is justified by faith without the deeds of the law" (Romans 3:28).

Not under the law but under grace

Every born-again Christian is no longer under law, but under grace (see Romans 6:14). But what does it mean to be "under grace," and how does it affect our lives as Christians? First, we must clearly understand what the Bible means by the terms *under law* and *under grace*.

Under law. The word *under* means "to be ruled, or dominated, by." So to be "under law" means to be ruled or dominated by the law. It means that our standing before God is based on our performance in terms of the law, the revelation of God's express will. Being "under law" means justifying ourselves in God's presence by our behavior regarding the law. The law always comes to us and says, "Do this, don't do that, and you shall live" (see Romans 10:5). Failure to keep the law results in the curse: "Cursed is everyone that continueth not in all things which are written in the book of the law to do them" (Galatians 3:10).

In the Garden of Eden, before sin, Adam and Eve were "under law." God created them with a perfect, sinless nature, and placed them under the law. "And the Lord God commanded the man, saying, Of every tree of the garden thou mayest freely eat: But of the tree of the knowledge of good and evil, thou shalt not eat of it: for in the day that thou eatest thereof thou shalt surely die" (Genesis 2:16, 17). When Adam and Eve disobeyed this command, they came under the condemnation of death; they forfeited their lives. This death sentence has passed to all humanity because all mankind was in Adam when he sinned and therefore was implicated in his sin (see Romans 5:12; 1 Corinthians 15:22).

Being "under law" also means being under the curse or condemnation of the law. This, too, is our plight; we are "by nature the children of wrath" (Ephesians 2:3). No matter how good an opinion we may have of ourselves, the fact is that we were born into a lost race. As Paul says, "Now we know that what things soever the law saith, it saith to them who are under the law: that every mouth may be stopped, and all the world may become guilty before God. Therefore by the deeds of the law there shall no flesh [person] be justified in his sight: for by the law is the knowledge of sin" (Romans 3:19, 20).

Paul is telling us in these verses that not only do we stand condemned under the law, but also that we cannot possibly meet its demands. To save us from this hopeless situation, "God sent forth his Son, made of a woman, made under the law, to redeem them that were under the law, that we might receive the adoption of sons" (Galatians 4:4, 5). In redeeming us from being "under law," Christ has put us "under grace." This is the position of all who have received Him by faith (see Romans 6:14).

Under grace. The word *grace* means a favor done for someone who doesn't deserve it. In spiritual terms, the New Testament defines grace primarily as God's loving disposition toward sinners that caused Him to give "his only begotten Son, that whosoever believeth on him should not perish, but have everlasting life" (John 3:16). The apostle Paul describes grace in these words: "In whom [Christ] we have redemption through his blood, the forgiveness of sins, according to the riches of his grace" (Ephesians 1:7). Since by nature fallen humanity is God's enemy, what He has done in saving us in His Son becomes more than merely a free gift; it becomes grace. It is by grace that we are saved (see Ephesians 2:8, 9; Romans 5:6-10). This is why the gospel is unconditional good news.

What does it mean to be "under grace"?

As we have seen, all mankind was born "in Adam" and is therefore born "under law," and "the law hath dominion over a man as long as he liveth" (Romans 7:1). But Christ united Himself with us in the incarnation and on the cross, so that we have become dead to the law's dominion "by the body of Christ" (Romans 7:4). In His resurrection, Christ raised us up with Him in His eternal life, born anew "unto a lively hope" (1 Peter 1:3), married to Christ, the second husband, and therefore we are now under His dominion. This is what it means to be "under grace."

As Christians, then, we are no longer under the law in the sense that our justification or salvation depends on our own self-motivated attempts to obey the law. (Of course, this *is* precisely the condition of all those who have not received Christ as their personal Saviour.) Those who have believed, who by faith have become one with Christ, are no longer under the law but under grace. Christ has become the fulfillment, the completion, of all that the law requires of us for righteousness (see Romans 10:4).

To be "under grace," then, is the exact opposite of being "under law." Under grace, we are no longer justified before God on the basis of our actions—the works of the law. We are justified entirely on the basis of what Christ has already done in His life, death, and resurrection. Christ's perfect righteousness, which He obtained in His humanity as our Substitute, justifies us. By His positive obedience to the law, and by His death, which met the justice of the law, Christ became righteousness forever to all who will accept His saving grace (see Romans 5:17).

Further, to be "under grace" means we have died to the life of sin, that our lives are now hidden in Christ (see Colossians 3:3). Christ's death on the cross was a corporate death in which all mankind died in the one Man (see 2 Corinthians 5:14). Therefore, when we by faith identify ourselves with this death, we become dead to sin and the law's dominion and become alive unto God. This is what our baptism signifies—our union with Christ crucified, buried, and resurrected. The result is that now, under grace, we walk in newness of life (see Romans 6:3, 4). This is what it means to be "under grace," and all this has important implications for how we live.

Living under grace

Being "under grace" delivers us from being "under law," but this does not at all mean that the law has been done away with. Anyone who believes or teaches so is perverting the gospel. Justification by faith does not abolish the law; it establishes it (see Romans 3:31).

God's law is as everlasting as Himself, for it is His self-sacrificing love set down in a written legal form (see Matthew 22:36-40; Romans 13:8, 10; Galatians 5:13, 14). In His Sermon on the Mount, Jesus Himself declared that He had not come to abolish the law.

Verily I say unto you, Till heaven and earth pass, one jot or one tittle shall in no wise pass from the law, till all be fulfilled. Whosoever therefore shall break one of these least commandments, and shall teach men so, he shall be called the least in the kingdom of heaven: but whosoever shall do and teach them, the same shall be called great in the kingdom of heaven (Matthew 5:18, 19).

When we were "under law," the problem we faced was not with the law, but with ourselves. The law is holy, just, and good (see Romans 7:12). The fault lies in us, because by nature we are carnal, sold as slaves under sin (see verse 14). God's holy law and our sinful natures are incompatible. "The carnal [flesh-controlled] mind . . . is not subject to the law of God, neither indeed can be" (Romans 8:7). That is why the first covenant, the old covenant, was faulty.

For finding fault with *them* [the Israelites], he [God] saith, . . . I will make a new covenant with the house of Israel and with the house of Judah: not according to the covenant that I made with their fathers in the day when I took them by the hand to lead them out of the land of Egypt; because they continued not in my covenant. . . . For this is the covenant that I will make with the house of Israel after those days, saith the Lord; I will put my laws into their mind, and write them in their hearts: and I will be to them a God, and they shall be to me a people (Hebrews 8:8-10, emphasis supplied).

So Christ did not abolish the law on the cross. Instead, He saved us from being under the law. He put an end to our corporate sinful lives that stood condemned under the law. In the resurrection, He raised us from death with a new life, the life of the Spirit, that is in perfect harmony with the law. This is the life He lived in His humanity, a life that perfectly obeyed God's holy law by the power of the Spirit. The law was never given as a *means* of salvation, but it will always be the *standard* of Christian living.

Jesus died once unto sin, but He was resurrected to live unto God (see Romans 6:10). In verse 11, Paul applies this same truth to the baptized believer: "Likewise, reckon [consider] ye also yourselves to be dead indeed unto sin, but alive unto God through Jesus Christ our Lord."

On what basis are we to consider ourselves dead to sin and alive to God?

On the basis of what God did to us in the humanity of Christ. By sheer grace He put us into Christ at the incarnation when divinity was united to our corporate humanity (see 1 Corinthians 1:30). That meant that when Christ died to sin, so did we—in Him. Thus the cross becomes God's power unto salvation from sin (see 1 Corinthians 1:18) as well as salvation from the dominion of the law (see Romans 7:4-6). Note how Paul applies this truth to his own life:

> So far as the Law is concerned, however, I am dead—killed by the Law itself—in order that I might live for God. I have been put to death with Christ on his cross, so that it is no longer I who live, but it is Christ who lives in me. This life that I live now, I live by faith in the Son of God, who loved me and gave his life for me (Galatians 2:19, 20, TEV).

So the first thing we need to understand about living under grace is that the law has not been abolished. And the second point is related to the first: Because Christians are "under grace" doesn't mean that they are free to live as they please. Grace does not give us any such liberty.

While we were under the law, we were subject to its authority. It demanded certain things of us, and we were obliged to meet those demands or suffer the penalty. So now, under grace, we are just as surely subject to the dominion and authority of grace. This means that our relationship is to Christ, the source of grace, and we must live under His authority. Christ is both Saviour and Lord. How does this affect us as far as Christian living is concerned? As Paul would say, "Much in every way." Here are two examples from Paul:

> What then? Shall we sin, because we are not under the law, but under grace? God forbid. Know ye not, that to whom ye yield yourselves servants to obey, his servants ye are to whom ye obey; whether of sin unto death, or of obedience unto righteousness? But God be thanked, that ye were the servants of sin, but ye have obeyed from the heart that form of doctrine which was delivered you. Being then made free

from sin, ye became the servants of righteousness (Romans 6:15-18).

> For brethren, ye have been called unto liberty; only use not liberty for an occasion to the flesh, but by love serve one another. For all the law is fulfilled in one word, even in this; Thou shalt love thy neighbor as thyself (Galatians 5:13, 14; cf. 1 Peter 2:15-19).

Clearly then, to live under grace means to allow Christ to live in us through faith. This is what Jesus was talking about in John 15:4, 5.

> Abide in me, and I in you. As the branch cannot bear fruit of itself, except it abide in the vine; no more can ye, except ye abide in me. I am the vine, ye are the branches: He that abideth in me, and I in him, the same bringeth forth much fruit: for without me ye can do nothing.

The third important thing we need to understand about living "under grace" concerns motivation.

Our old relationship under the law may be described as a relationship of fear. This is because the law can never sympathize with our weakness and inability to meet its demands. Neither is the law able to help us meet its requirements. It can only demand obedience and condemn us every time we fail. So our situation under the law was to be always in bondage to fear of death (see Hebrews 2:15).

How different is our situation under grace! Unlike the law, Christ understands our weakness and our inability to be truly good. He is able to sympathize with us in our struggles against temptation. He was made like us in all things and was tempted in all points like us; He understands and sympathizes and is able to help us (see Hebrews 2:17, 18; 4:15).

But even more than this: He has delivered us from it all. He has delivered us from the fear of death because He died for us (see Hebrews 2:14, 15). He has delivered us from the fear of slavery to sin because He condemned sin in the flesh—our flesh (see Romans 6:22; 8:2, 3). He has reconciled us to God so that we have the blessed hope of heaven and eternal life; we can call God "Dear Father" (see Galatians 4:4-6). All these are our privileges "under grace." And this means that we no longer serve God according to the letter (out of fear), but according to the spirit (out of a heartfelt gratitude for Christ) (see Romans 7:6).

Under grace, our relationship is one of love and appreciation—not a relationship of fear such as we experience under the law. Fear of punishment no longer motivates our actions; instead, love for God compels us to do right and live for Him (see 2 Corinthians 5:14, 15). Jesus said, "If ye love me, keep my commandments" (John 14:15; cf. 1 John 5:3).

Being under grace also frees us from the self-centered motivation of trying to do right in order to receive a reward. Neither fear of punishment nor hope of a reward in heaven is a strong enough motivation to enable us to obey the "works of the law." But when we understand and appreciate the *agape* love that led the Son of God to the cross for us, we gladly will serve Him and others with no thought of self or reward.

Sinning under grace

One of the main concerns haunting Christians is this: If we continue to sin even after we are under grace, how does this affect our relationship with God? Do we lose our justification every time we sin? Do we, therefore, need to be reconverted after each failure or otherwise be eternally lost?

Some believe that the answer is Yes. But those who believe such a "yo-yo" doctrine of salvation have failed to understand God's unconditional *agape* love and the biblical meaning of being saved by grace.

According to Paul, it is impossible for someone who truly understands salvation by grace, and who appreciates Christ's cross, to go on condoning sin (see Romans 6:1, 2). Righteousness is by faith, and if the faith is there, the righteousness is sure to be there as well—and there is no sin in righteousness (see Romans 6:14-18).

When Paul declared in Romans 6:14, "Sin shall not have dominion over you: for ye are not under law, but under grace," he didn't mean that a believer *cannot* sin, but that sin no longer has authority to condemn or control a believer, because such a person is no longer under the law's control but under grace. In 1 Corinthians 15:56, Paul says, "The sting of death is sin; and the strength of sin is the law." He means that sin itself has no power to destroy a person unless the authority of the law is present to condemn. Since a believer is no longer under the law's authority, sin can no longer bring upon the believer the law's condemnation of eternal death. The believer is delivered from the power of sin.

Misuse of grace

"Wait a minute!" you object. "That is a dangerous teaching; it will lead to loose living!"

Your fears, of course, are absolutely correct. Because of our sinful condition, the gospel is not only good news, it is also dangerous news. When faith becomes a counterfeit, it can easily be perverted into a license to sin, as was the case with the Christians to whom James wrote (see James 2:19-26).

Because believers are no longer under the law, and because grace abounds much more than does sin, can Christians condone continuing to sin while under grace? That is the big question Paul presents to his readers in Romans 6. And his answer is an emphatic *NO!* In fact, Paul spends all of Romans chapter 6 warning Christians against the attitude that because they are under grace it doesn't matter if they go on sinning.

What reasons does Paul give why Christians under grace must not give place to sin?

First, because in Christ we have died to sin. That is, we have terminated our relationship with it (see verses 2, 11). Second, by our own choice we have become slaves of God, who is the author of righteousness—not sin (see verse 17). On these two grounds, the doctrine of salvation by grace will not permit a Christian to continue to cherish sin.

Obviously, this does not mean that we never stumble and fall. As babes in Christ, we know that failure to live up to God's ideal is a problem in Christian living. Because we have not yet learned to fully understand the gospel or to walk unceasingly by the Spirit, we fall all too often. But how do such failures affect our relationship with God? That question continues to demand an answer.

There is a world of difference between sinning under law and sinning under grace. To understand the difference, let's look at the contrast between the law as a written code and Christ as a living reality. When we compare them, we will discover that in one sense they are the same, yet in another sense, they are exact opposites.

For instance, the spirit behind the law is love (see Matthew 22:36-40). So it can be identified with Christ, who is love (see 1 John 4:8; Ephesians 5:1, 2). However, when we look at the law itself as a written code, it becomes a set of rules legally binding on human beings. As such, it cannot sympathize with our weak condition or help us. All it can do is command obedience and condemn every failure (see Galatians 3:10).

On the contrary, Christ is a person who feels and understands our struggles; He is able to help us because He Himself was tempted in all points like us except that He conquered every temptation (see Hebrews 4:15). In this sense, the law and Christ differ radically.

All this throws an important light on the matter of sinning. When we sinned before accepting God's redemptive grace in Christ, we recognized only that we had sinned against the law, against a moral code or a set of rules. The result we feared was the punishment specified by the law (see Romans 1:18; Galatians 3:10). But now that we are believers and no longer under the law, but under grace, we do not sin merely against a set of rules. When we sin now, we realize that we sin against a Person "who loved [us], and gave himself for [us]" (Galatians 2:20). This makes a tremendous difference in our attitude toward sin.

Let's say you are driving along the highway faster than the speed limit, when a police officer stops you. You plead for mercy, confessing your sorrow for speeding. What is your motivation? If you've ever found yourself in this situation, I think you'll agree with me that your confession and repentance are motivated by selfish concerns and not by love for the speed limit or the police officer who represents the law.

Then you drive home (more slowly, of course), and there you unintentionally do something to offend your husband or wife, whom you love and who loves you dearly. Immediately you are sorry for what you have done; you confess in repentance. What is your motivation now? Not fear of punishment. You are sorry because you have hurt someone dear to you. That is the difference between sinning under law and sinning under grace. Incidentally, this was the difference between the repentance of Judas, who betrayed Christ, and the repentance of Peter, who denied Him. Judas was motivated by self; Peter by love. Those who sin under the law can repent only in terms of a fear of punishment or a desire for reward—both self-centered concerns. Under grace, repentance and confession result from a love relationship with Christ. We are constantly aware of what our sins did to Christ on the cross—they killed Him there! How, then, can a Christian under grace condone sin? That would mean deliberately crucifying Christ, and that is unthinkable to anyone who appreciates God's "unspeakable gift" (2 Corinthians 9:15).

We Christians must learn to hate sin, not because we fear that sinning will deprive us of heaven but because our sins put Christ on the cross and continue to put Him to an open shame (see Galatians 3:13; Hebrews 6:4-6). A legalist does not hate sin; he hates the punishment for sin. Such a religion is only paganism in Christian dress.

Because God could not save us by simply ignoring the demands of His holy law, salvation from sin is costly. The wages of sin is death (see Ezekiel 18:20; Romans 6:23), and in order to save us from the condemnation of the law, God had to meet its just demands. He did this when He laid upon Christ, our Substitute, the iniquity of us all and offered Him up on the cross as the only valid sacrifice for our sins (see Isaiah 53:6, 10, 11).

So, what about our question? How do our failures and sins, even after we are under grace, affect our relationship with God?

Stumbling under grace, falling into sin, does not deprive us of justification. Neither does it bring condemnation. But if we have begun to appreciate the terrible cost of our salvation, such failures do create a deeper hatred for sin. We realize that every sin we commit was vitally involved in Christ's death on the cross.

Key Points in Chapter 16
Law and Grace—I

1. On the surface, law and grace seem antagonistic toward each other. The law demands obedience as a condition of salvation (see Romans 10:5), while grace offers salvation as a free gift without works (see Ephesians 2:8, 9).

2. The Bible teaches that every born-again Christian is no longer "under law" but "under grace" (see Romans 6:14).

    a. To be "under law" means to be ruled by the law. It means that our standing before God is based on our performance in terms of the law. Being "under law" also means being subject to the condemnation of the law.

    b. To be "under grace" is the exact opposite of being "under law." Under grace, we are justified entirely on the basis of what Christ has done in His life, death, and resurrection. To be "under grace" means that we have died "in Christ" to the life of sin and that our lives are now hidden in Christ (see Colossians 3:3).

3. Being "under grace" does *not* mean that the law has been done away with in our experience. Justification by faith does not abolish the law—it establishes it.

4. When we were "under law," the problem we faced was not with the law, but with ourselves. The law is holy, just, and good. We are carnal, sold as slaves under sin (see Romans 7:12, 14).

5. The law was never given as a means of salvation, but it will always be the standard of Christian living. Grace does not give us the liberty to live as we please.

6. To live "under grace" means to allow Christ to live in us through faith.

7. "Under law," the motivation for obedience is fear of punishment. "Under grace," the motivation for obedience is love and appreciation.

8. If we sin "under grace," we do not lose our justification. However, sincere Christians cannot condone continuing to sin while "under grace."

9. We must learn to hate sin, not because we fear that it will deprive us of heaven but because our sins put Christ on the cross and continue to put Him to open shame (see Galatians 3:13; Hebrews 6:4-6).

Chapter Seventeen

Law and Grace
II

One reason so many Christians are confused about their salvation under grace is that they fail to realize that the New Testament speaks of two aspects of salvation. We studied this topic earlier in this book, yet because so many Christians are trapped in a subtle form of legalism, we need to review these two aspects very briefly here.

Two aspects of salvation

The first aspect of salvation is what God did in Christ some two thousand years ago; the second is what God is doing now in every believer and will bring to completion at the second coming. The New Testament refers to the first phase as "you in Christ" and to the second as "Christ in you" (see John 15:4, 5). These two aspects are related like two sides of a coin, yet they are also distinct in at least four areas.

1. *Complete versus progressive.* What God did in Christ—the objective facts of the gospel—is a finished work. In Him we stand perfect, provided with every spiritual blessing pertaining to heaven (see Ephesians 1:3; Colossians 2:10). In contrast, what God is doing in us—the subjective experience of the gospel—is something that continues through life and will continue until the second coming (see Philippians 3:12-14; Romans 8:24, 25). This is the aspect of salvation you see on some bumper stickers—"Be

patient: God isn't finished with me yet!"

2. *Universal versus individual.* What God did in Christ applies to all mankind, so that in Him the whole world stands legally justified. This is the unconditional good news of the gospel (see Romans 5:18; 1 John 2:2). What God does in us, on the other hand, applies only to the individual, born-again Christian who by faith has accepted Jesus Christ as his or her Saviour (see Romans 8:9, 10; Ephesians 3:17).

3. *Divine and human.* God's saving activity in Christ is a work He accomplished entirely without human help (see Romans 3:21; Philippians 3:9). In contrast, God's work in us involves our cooperation. That is why we are admonished to "walk in the Spirit" (Galatians 5:16) or to "put on the Lord Jesus Christ" (Romans 13:14) or to "abide in me" (John 15:4).

4. *Saving and witnessing.* The righteousness God obtained for all humanity in Christ is full of merit. It is this alone that qualifies us for heaven, now and in the judgment (see Ephesians 2:8, 9; Titus 3:5). The righteousness God produces in us, on the other hand, has no saving value. Rather, it is the fruit of justification by faith and demonstrates and witnesses to the righteousness that we have already received in Christ by faith (see Ephesians 2:10; Titus 3:8).

This is an important distinction, especially since so many look to their own performance for the assurance of salvation. Our righteous performance, even though it is of God and is pleasing to Him, does not contribute in the slightest toward our title to heaven. Our performance is important, however, since it is the most effective witness of God's saving power. As the pagan philosopher Nietzsche once said, "If you Christians expect me to believe in your redeemer, you will have to look a lot more redeemed!"

Standing in grace

One of the great privileges we have as Christians is standing in grace (see Romans 5:1, 2). What does this mean?

It means that not only do we have peace with God and full assurance of salvation through the justification Christ obtained for all mankind, but that we also are now standing in a special way in God's realm of grace. Although we still possess sinful flesh, we have within us the indwelling Spirit, who is able to reproduce in us Christ's righteousness and to enable us to overcome every temptation. Through Christ, we possess the very life of God so that now He is able to work in us "both to will and to do of his good pleasure" (Philippians 2:13). Before, while living under law and in our own strength, we were always coming short of the glory of God (see Romans 3:23), but now, under grace, our situation has changed entirely so that we have the hope of experiencing God's glory—His life of self-sacrificing love (see 2 Corinthians 3:17, 18).

The apostle Paul often used the word *grace* in terms of the divine power that fitted him to do the work and will of God. "By the grace of God I am what I am: and his grace which was bestowed on me was not in vain; but I labored more abundantly than they all: yet not I, but the grace of God which was with me" (1 Corinthians 15:10; cf. 2 Corinthians 12:7-10; Ephesians 3:7, 8; 1 Timothy 1:14). This is what it means to stand in grace, and this privilege belongs to all believers.

During a Week of Prayer that I was conducting at a Christian college in Ethiopia, an Egyptian senior student asked me, "Is it a sin for Christians to bear arms for their country and kill?" He was soon returning to Egypt to serve in the army in his country's war with Israel.

"Do you know of any dead Egyptians fighting for their country?" I replied. I reminded him that, as a Christian, he was dead and his life was hidden with Christ (see Colossians 3:3). Unfortunately, he refused to accept this biblical fact. Two weeks later, he was pinned beneath the school's tractor in an accident and pronounced dead at a nearby mission hospital. Later, a nurse came to cover his body with a sheet. She saw his eyes blink and cried out, "He's alive!" It was a miracle in apparent answer to the prayers of his fellow students.

When I visited him in the hospital some days later, I asked, "How are you?"

Through bandaged lips, he whispered, "I am dead, and my life is hid in Christ."

I have always cherished that experience as an example of God's Spirit working in a human life. That is what it means to stand in God's grace.

Paul says that we Christians are not debtors to the flesh, to live according to it, but to the Spirit (see Romans 8:12, 13). In other words, we have no business trying to live—even trying to be good—in our natural strength and abilities. It is the Spirit of Christ who must live in us by faith. The life we now live in our bodies must be the life of Christ that we have received by faith (see Galatians 2:20). This is all part of God's program of being under grace.

The grace that has saved us from domination by the law will now continue to live in us and produce the fruits of the Spirit—"love, joy, peace, longsuffering, gentleness, goodness, faith, meekness, temperance" (Galatians 5:22, 23). Against such, "there is no law" (verse 24). These fruits are in harmony with God's law, so that under grace the law we could not keep in our natural strength is now actually being fulfilled in us (see Romans 8:4).

Of course, although we stand in God's realm of grace, we still live in this wicked world, and the law of sin still lives in our bodies (see Romans 7:22). But this law of sin should not *reign* in us or *dominate* us, because we now are under grace, not law (see Romans 6:12-14). In our own strength we are no match for the law, as Paul makes clear in Romans chapter 7. But the power of grace is greater than all the power Satan can muster through our sinful flesh. "I can do all things through Christ which strengtheneth me" (Philippians 4:13).

To stand under grace, therefore, is to be under the reign of Christ's life—the life that has conquered and condemned sin in the flesh (see Romans 8:3). The law of sin that resides in our mortal bodies will always try to dominate us through the flesh. That is how we experience temptation (see James 1:14). Taking advantage of our sinful natures, Satan turns the natural, God-given desires of the body into lust. He tries to make us slaves to these desires rather than being their masters. But because we are under grace we possess the life and power of God through which we can "escape the corruption that is in the world through lust" (2 Peter 1:4). Daily, hourly, by faith we allow Christ to live in us and "make not provision for the flesh, to fulfill the lusts thereof" (Romans 13:14).

In becoming a Christian, we have undergone a radical change. "If any man be in Christ, he is a new creature: old things are passed away; behold, all things are become new" (2 Corinthians

5:17). Christians are not just people whose sins have been forgiven so that they may go to heaven. They are people in whom everything that once belonged to the old has passed away. Our old position under the law, our old lives of sin, all have passed away on the cross of Christ. Now, through His resurrection, we have become a new creation in a new position that is "under grace." We possess a new life; we are partakers of the divine nature (see 2 Peter 1:4). When we understand these truths and allow them to work in and through us, we will no longer behave as members of this world who are controlled by "the lust of the flesh, the lust of the eyes, and the pride of life" (1 John 2:16). We will act as sons and daughters of God. We will be walking in the Spirit, reflecting the character of Christ.

The law as a standard

In light of all this, how should we Christians view the law? Is it still binding on us?

The answer is most emphatically *No*; the law is not binding on us *as a means of salvation*. But the answer is a most definite *Yes* if we are speaking of the law *as a standard for Christian living*.

One reason for the misunderstanding and antagonism about the law among so many sincere Christians is a failure to understand what the apostle Paul has said about the law. On the one hand, he makes statements that appear on the surface to imply that the law is abolished (see Romans 7:1-10; Galatians 2:19; 2 Corinthians 3:4-17; Ephesians 2:14-16). We can quote other statements, however, to prove that Paul upheld the same law and totally rejected the idea that faith abolishes it (see Romans 3:31; 7:12-22; 13:8-10; Galatians 5:13, 14).

How can we solve this apparent contradiction? Much of our problem understanding all that Paul has to say about "law" comes from our failure to realize that in Greek he had no separate word or phrase to denote what we, today, call "legalism." Therefore, Paul used the same term for both his positive references to God's law (which he upheld) and his negative statements about the law when it was used by human beings to produce their own righteousness (which he condemned).

If we read Paul carefully, we will find that he upheld the law as the standard of Christian living, but he condemned anyone who used it as a substitute for faith or as a means to gain that righteousness which can come only from God. In studying what Paul has to say about the law, it's helpful to note that when he is condemning what we call "legalism," he often uses the phrase translated in the King James Version of the Bible as "works of the law" (see Romans 3:20; 9:30-32; Galatians 2:16; 3:1.)

Falling from grace

Too many Christians believe that once a person is saved in Christ through faith, nothing at all can remove that salvation from such a person. This is a great deception.

True, the *righteousness* that saves us is always in Christ, and since He is in heaven, where no thief can enter, it cannot be touched. But the *faith* that makes that righteousness effective is in us, and we can renounce or forsake it. That is why the Scriptures so often admonish us to hold fast to our faith at all cost (see Matthew 10:22; Acts 20:24; 1 Corinthians 15:58; Galatians 6:9; Hebrews 3:6; 4:14; 10:23).

Each person who becomes a Christian automatically becomes a traitor to Satan, the prince of this world. Satan will not willingly lose one of his subjects, so he increases his efforts sevenfold to regain that person (see Matthew 12:43-45). How does he do this? Satan uses three primary methods to tempt a believer to fall from grace. He will try any, or all, that he thinks necessary.

1. *Perverting the gospel.* Satan's first method is to misrepresent some aspect of gospel truth so that he succeeds in turning our eyes from Christ to self. He makes it appear that salvation comes not by faith alone, but that it depends to some degree on our own behavior. He used this successfully with the Galatian Christians (see Galatians 1:6, 7; 3:1-3). But Satan cannot confuse us if we will simply believe the truth Paul pointed out to those in Galatia who were in danger of falling away from grace:

> Christ is become of no effect unto you, whosoever of you are justified by the law; ye are fallen from grace. For we through the Spirit wait for the hope of righteousness by faith. For in Jesus Christ neither circumcision availeth anything, nor uncircumcision; but faith which worketh by love (Galatians 5:4-6).

To be under grace means that Christ is our righteousness in every way and in every sense of the word. Through the gospel, we receive Christ's righteousness both as an objective fact (imputed righteousness) and as a subjective experience (imparted righteousness). Both are received by faith alone, and nothing must be added to our faith (see Romans 1:17). Anyone who tries to justify himself before God in the slightest by his own actions is actually denying that Christ is his righteousness. He is fallen from grace.

We simply cannot have it both ways. We cannot receive Christ by faith, acknowledge that we are spiritually bankrupt and cannot save ourselves, and then claim that we can save ourselves by somehow having our good works add something toward our salvation. This subtle form of legalism puts us in danger of losing Christ entirely.

Salvation is not partly from Christ and partly from ourselves. To be under law or under grace are opposites that cannot be mixed. Either we receive Christ by faith as our total righteousness both in terms of our standing before God and in our daily living, or we must try to justify ourselves entirely by our own law keeping, which is impossible. It is either one or the other; we cannot have some of both.

2. *Love of this world.* This is Satan's second method to cause believers to fall from grace. He dangles the trinkets of this world before us and tries to gradually draw us back into the world and away from Christ. This was what happened to Demas. Paul wrote that Demas "hath forsaken me, having loved this present world" (2 Timothy 4:10). Money, self-glory, position, pleasures of the flesh—these are but some of Satan's bait. Our way of escape is to keep ever before us "the unsearchable riches of Christ" (Ephesians 3:8) as demonstrated on the cross.

Even if we have experienced salvation by faith in Christ, this does not mean that our eternal destiny is secure. Only those whose faith endures to the end will receive the crown of life (see Mark 13:13; James 1:12). If our hold on Christ is weak, we can be drawn away (see Matthew 13:22), and thus faith becomes a fight to the end (see 1 Timothy 6:12).

Of course, as long as we are united to Christ by faith, our salvation is secure. But this does not mean that our faith itself is secure. Unless we allow it to grow through Bible study, prayer, fellowship, and witnessing, we will find ourselves vulnerable to Satan's attacks. He will continue to try to snatch us out of Christ if possible. A believer can most certainly forsake Christ and the church and return to the world. He or she can fall from grace and be lost (see Hebrews 6:4-6). But even then, the Saviour still loves that lost sheep and seeks to restore it to the fold.

3. *Persecution.* The devil may use this third method to cause us to fall from grace. The flesh does not like suffering, and Satan is well aware of this. He may bring persecution in various ways— physical, social, or mental. But, again, Satan can never be success- ful if we prize "fellowship" with Christ in His sufferings (see Philippians 3:10).

Persecution may come from the world or even from our own families or the church. Mistreatment, discrimination, or unfair practices in the church can cause us to become so discouraged or filled with self-pity that we become targets for Satan's attacks. He will try to manipulate us to fight the church, then leave it and become its enemy.

Satan may persecute us by making life extremely difficult. The temptation is to compromise with truth, and the result is to slowly lose one's grip on Christ. We can overcome this temptation if we remember our Saviour led a difficult life as well; He had not so much as a place to lay His head (see Matthew 8:20).

The hostility of the world may include even the threat of death. Paul warned Timothy, "All that will live godly in Christ Jesus shall suffer persecution" (2 Timothy 3:12). And Peter counseled his readers,

Be sober, be vigilant; because your adversary the devil, as a roaring lion, walketh about, seeking whom he may devour: Whom resist steadfast in the faith, knowing that the same afflictions are accomplished in your brethren that are in the world (1 Peter 5:8, 9).

Finally, a scriptural warning about the consequences of falling from grace: "The just shall live by faith: but if any man draw back my soul shall have no pleasure in him" (Hebrews 10:38). But this warning need not apply to any of us, for verse 39 goes on to say,

"We are not of them who draw back unto perdition: but of them that believe to the saving of the soul."

As we rejoice in the wonderful truth of salvation by grace in Christ, may

> the very God of peace sanctify you wholly; and I pray God your whole spirit and soul and body be preserved blameless unto the coming of our Lord Jesus Christ. Faithful is he that calleth you, who also will do it. . . . The grace of our Lord Jesus Christ be with you. Amen (1 Thessalonians 5:23, 24, 28).

Key Points in Chapter 17
Law and Grace—II

1. As Christians, we stand in grace. This means that although we still possess sinful flesh, we have within us the indwelling Spirit, who is able to reproduce in us Christ's righteousness and to enable us to overcome every temptation.

2. Christians are not just people whose sins have been forgiven so they can go to heaven. They are people in whom everything that once belonged to the old life has passed away on the cross of Christ.

3. Is the law binding on such Christians? It is not binding on us as a means of salvation, but it most certainly is binding on us as a standard for Christian living.

4. Can a person who is saved in Christ through faith ever lose that salvation? Yes. The righteousness that saves us is in Christ and cannot be touched, but the faith that makes that righteousness effective is in us, and we can renounce or forsake it.

5. Satan uses three main methods to tempt a believer to fall from grace:

   a. *Perverting the gospel.* Satan tries to make us believe that salvation is not entirely by faith alone, but that it depends to some degree upon our behavior.

   b. *Love of this world.* Satan dangles the trinkets of the world before us and tries to draw us back into the world and away from Christ.

   c. *Persecution.* The flesh does not like suffering, and Satan takes advantage of this. He brings physical, mental, or social persecution to try to break our hold on Christ.

Chapter Eighteen

The Sabbath Rest

The Sabbath is more than a day of physical and mental relaxation. It is even more than the day on which we worship. The Sabbath has a definite redemptive significance—a distinct connection with the everlasting gospel.

The New Testament often uses the word *rest* to describe the good news of salvation realized in the holy history of Jesus Christ (see Matthew 11:28; Hebrews 4:2, 3). Ever since the Fall, this promised saving rest in Christ has been linked with the Sabbath. That is why the major feast days in the Old Testament were designated as Sabbath days of rest—they pointed ahead to the Messiah and His redemptive activity.

The significance of the Sabbath to God

The word *sabbath* means "rest," and the first thing we discover about it in the Old Testament is that the Sabbath day belongs to God. He calls it "my holy day" (Isaiah 58:13); "my sabbaths" (Exodus 31:13). "The seventh day is the sabbath of the Lord thy God" (Exodus 20:10). Since the Sabbath clearly belongs to God, it is unscriptural to refer to it as the "Jewish Sabbath." Yes, it was made for man (see Mark 2:27), but it does not belong to man—Jew or Gentile. It belongs to God.

The next logical question is: Why would an almighty God, who obviously doesn't need to rest, set aside the seventh day as His special day of rest? Scripture's answer to this question is that God set aside this Sabbath day, this day of rest, to signify His perfect and finished work of creation (see Genesis 1:31; 2:1-3; Hebrews 4:4). This fact becomes extremely important to our understanding of the gospel.

We must keep in mind that this Sabbath is *God's* seventh day, not ours. God took six days to create everything that goes to make up our planet. Then He set aside (sanctified) the seventh day as His Sabbath (see Exodus 20:11). Adam and Eve were created at the very end of the sixth day (see Genesis 1:26-31). Therefore, God's seventh-day Sabbath was actually mankind's first whole day. Let me explain why I believe this is important, especially when we consider the Sabbath in light of our redemption in Christ.

God worked for six days in creating this world. Only when His work was perfect and complete did He rest (see Genesis 2:1-3). Adam and Eve, on the other hand, did not begin by working; they spent their first whole day of life resting on God's Sabbath. Only after they had "entered" into God's rest did they follow it with six days of work. Mankind began by first receiving God's handiwork as an entirely free gift, and only then could humanity enjoy His creation during the rest of the week.

Like creation, salvation begins, not by doing something, but by resting in the perfect, finished work Jesus accomplished in His doing and dying. Just as Adam and Eve spent their first day in Sabbath rest before taking up their work, we can enjoy the blessings of salvation only by first resting in the completed righteousness Jesus has provided. From this perspective, the Sabbath rest becomes the very foundation of the glorious truth of righteousness by faith.

When He set apart, or sanctified, the Sabbath, God was entering into an everlasting covenant relationship with mankind—a relationship in which men and women were always to be dependent on Him. Thus, when Adam and Eve sinned, choosing to be self-dependent rather than God-dependent, they broke this God-given covenant. One result was that they forfeited the true rest that the Sabbath symbolized. "In the sweat of thy face shalt thou eat bread" (Genesis 3:19). But Jesus came into this world for the express purpose of restoring this rest that mankind lost at the Fall (see Matthew 11:28). In doing this, He restored the significance of the Sabbath. In order to receive the good news of salvation, we must return to this fundamental principle of Sabbath rest that was given to our first parents.

The New Testament makes it clear that Jesus Christ was the agent through whom God accomplished both creation (see John 1:3; Ephesians 3:9; Colossians 1:16; Revelation 3:14) and redemption (see John 3:16, 17; Romans 3:24; 1 Corinthians 1:30; Galatians 3:13; Colossians 1:14; Titus 2:14; Hebrews 9:12; 1 Peter 1:18; Revelation 5:9). Just as Christ finished creation at the end of the sixth day and rested the seventh, so He also finished redemption on the cross on the sixth day and rested in the tomb the seventh day (see John 17:4; 19:30).

Further, Christ's work of restoration, which will be realized at the end of His heavenly ministry (see 1 Corinthians 15:24-26; Hebrews 2:13), is also linked with the Sabbath (see Isaiah 66:22, 23). His work of restoration will be a perfect, finished work as were creation and redemption. So the Sabbath has a threefold significance to us—creation, redemption, and restoration.

Because Christ is our Creator, Redeemer, and Restorer, He has the perfect right to claim the title "Lord of the Sabbath day" (see Mark 2:28; Luke 6:5; Revelation 1:10). When the Jewish nation rejected Him as the Messiah, their Sabbath keeping lost its meaning. That is why Hebrews says, "There remaineth therefore a rest [*sabbatismos*, a "sabbath-keeping rest"] to the people of God" (Hebrews 4:9). Any Sabbath keeping that is not motivated by a faith response to Christ's perfect atonement on the cross is a sham and still belongs to the old covenant of salvation by works.

The significance of the Sabbath to man

God created the world through Christ for our benefit. We made no contribution to creation; we only received it as a gift of God. Although the Sabbath belongs to God, as we have seen, He made it, like the world, for our benefit (see Exodus 31:13; Ezekiel 20:12; Mark 2:27). God set apart, or sanctified, the Sabbath rest to remind us that He is our loving provider and that we are dependent on Him for all our needs.

It's significant that God made this Sabbath covenant with mankind before the Fall. So, had Adam and Eve never sinned, we would still be keeping God's Sabbath as a day of rest. When sin entered the world, however, it destroyed God's original significance for Sabbath rest. Sin is rebellion against our dependence on God and a demand to be dependent only on self (see Romans 1:21; Philippians 2:21). Therefore, when sin separated us from God (see Isaiah 59:2), the Sabbath could no longer have the same significance for us. Mankind had to introduce his own rest day, Sunday. Unlike God's rest day, however, man's substitute day does not point to a perfect, finished work—either of creation or redemption. This fact is very important in light of the final showdown that will occur in the great controversy between salvation by faith, symbolized by God's Sabbath, versus salvation by works, symbolized by man's Sunday.

At the cross, Jesus Christ accomplished a perfect, finished redemption on the sixth day, just as He had completed a perfect work of creation at the end of the sixth day (see Luke 23:54). In this way He restored the Sabbath rest that He had given at Eden and that had been marred by sin. Now, all who receive the gospel by faith once again enter into God's saving rest, of which the Sabbath is a sign (see Hebrews 4:2, 3; cf. Exodus 31:13; Ezekiel 20:12; Isaiah 58:13, 14). In His Sermon on the Mount, Christ clearly taught that if we first seek His kingdom and His righteousness (which is by faith), all our needs will be supplied (see Matthew 6:33).

In other words, the gospel has made a way of escape for us from self-dependence, which is the source of all our problems, to God-dependence, which is the source of all our joy and happiness. But one thing is sure—we cannot serve two masters; we cannot serve self and God (Matthew 6:24-34). When we enter into God's rest, His day of rest must become our day of rest. This is the outward sign that we have chosen to live by faith alone. Keeping the Sabbath from this motivation of faith is true Sabbath keeping.

The law and the Sabbath

Before we can consider the Sabbath in relationship to God's law, we must first remind ourselves that God never gave the law as a means of salvation (see Romans 3:28; Galatians 2:16). This is the error the Jews made, the error of the old covenant that ended in miserable failure (see Romans 9:30-33; Hebrews 8:7-11). Therefore, anyone who keeps God's Sabbath in order to be saved is repeating the mistake of the Jews and is perverting the very purpose of the Sabbath rest. When we make Sabbath keeping a requirement for salvation, we are not entering rest at all. We are not pointing to a finished, complete salvation. Instead, we are turning the Sabbath into the very opposite of what God intended it to be; we are making it into a means of salvation by works. Such Sabbath keeping is meaningless.

How, then, should a Christian, who has been saved by grace through faith alone, keep the Sabbath?

The New Testament, especially the apostle Paul, clearly teaches that God never gave His law as a method of salvation. In fact, before God gave the Jews His law on Mount Sinai, He stated, "I am the Lord thy God, which have brought thee out of the land of Egypt, out of the house of bondage" (Exodus 20:2). God first redeemed Israel and *then* gave the Israelites His law. Moses applied this principle specifically to Sabbath keeping (see Deuteronomy 5:15). Yet although God did not give us the law as a means of salvation, He certainly wants us to consider His law to be the standard for Christian living (see Romans 13:8-10; Galatians 5:13, 14; 1 John 5:1-3; 2 John 6).

The true motivation for keeping the law, Jesus said, was love (see Matthew 22:36-40; John 14:15). The Old Testament agreed (see Deuteronomy 6:5; Leviticus 19:18). Yet we cannot generate this love out of our own sinful natures, because it is the *agape* love, the self-sacrificing love, that originates with God. Therefore, God gives us this *agape* love as His gift to us through His Holy Spirit (see 1 Corinthians 12:31; 13:13). He doesn't give us this love so that it will flow back to Him; that would make God Himself self-centered! Rather, He gives us this unselfish love so that we can reflect it toward others as evidence of the saving power of the gospel over self (see John 13:34, 35; Romans 5:5; 2 Corinthians 5:14, 15). This is what it means to have the law written on our hearts (see Hebrews 8:10).

The first four of God's Ten Commandments have to do with our relationship to Him; the last six deal with our relationships with our neighbors. Since *agape* "seeketh not her own" (1 Corinthians 13:5), how do we obey the first four commandments without making God self-centered? We do so by remembering that the only way we can obey is through faith. As we obey the first four commandments by faith, the result is the new-birth experience, and with this experience comes the gift of *agape* love that enables us to keep the last six commandments of love for our neighbors.

The New Testament has little to say about our obeying the first four commandments, because all God wants from us, in regard to our relationship with Him, is faith (see John 6:28, 29; Hebrews 11:6; 1 John 3:23). He wants us to have a faith that is motivated by a heart appreciation for His supreme gift of love, Jesus Christ (see Galatians 5:6). So the only way we can acceptably keep the fourth commandment, the Sabbath commandment, is by faith—entering by faith into God's rest. The Sabbath becomes, in this context, the seal of righteousness by faith.

The Sabbath-Sunday controversy

The real issue is not the one we usually think of—Sabbath keeping versus Sunday keeping. Many sincere Sunday-keeping Christians today are fully resting in Christ for salvation. They are keeping the wrong day but for the right reason. Likewise, many sincere Sabbath-keeping Christians do so because they think their Sabbath keeping will save them. They are keeping the right day for the wrong reason. Both need to be corrected, and if we let Him, the Holy Spirit will do this as He guides us into all truth (see John 16:13).

When the gospel of the kingdom shall be preached in all the world for a witness to all nations (see Matthew 24:14), it will polarize the human race into only two camps—believers and unbelievers (see 1 John 5:19). There will be only those who are fully resting in Christ and those who have ultimately rejected Him. In the end time, all who come under the banner of Christ will worship the Lord of the Sabbath; their Sabbath keeping will be the outward sign or seal of the righteousness they have already received by faith, just as Abraham's circumcision was "a seal of the righteousness of the faith which he had yet being uncircumcised" (Romans 4:11).

In the end time, those who have deliberately turned their backs on God's free gift of salvation in Christ will worship the dragon that gives power to the beast (see Revelation 13:3, 4).

They will exalt Sunday as man's day of rest in defiance of God's rest day. The issue, then, in the final conflict will not be between two groups of Christians, or even between two rest days, but between two opposing methods of salvation. The conflict will be between the seventh-day Sabbath, signifying salvation by faith alone, and Sunday, signifying salvation by human effort.

The fundamental issue throughout Scripture is salvation by faith versus salvation by works. At the heart of the Bible message is salvation by grace made effective through faith alone (see Habakkuk 2:4; Romans 3:28; Galatians 2:16; Ephesians 2:8, 9; Hebrews 10:38, 39; Hebrews 11:1-40). At the heart of every false religion is salvation by works. In ancient times, Sunday became not only man's day of physical and mental rest, but above all it symbolized his day of spiritual rest and worship based on the pagan belief that the sun was the chief of gods. This became prominent in the Roman Empire of Christ's day. Hence, at its very foundation, Sunday rest is a pagan institution representing self-righteousness in contradiction to God's Sabbath, the sign of righteousness by faith. These two opposing concepts of salvation have been in conflict since the Fall and can never be reconciled.

When the true gospel of righteousness by faith will be fully recovered and preached in all the world for a witness, every person will have to make a choice—either for or against Christ (see Deuteronomy 30:19, 20; Joshua 24:13-15; Romans 9:30-33; Philippians 3:3-9). At that time, the Sabbath will become God's seal, representing righteousness by faith. Sunday keeping, in contrast, will represent the mark of the beast, signifying mankind's rejection of God's saving grace in Christ (see Revelation 14:10, 11). When laws legally establishing Sunday worship are enacted, it will indicate the world's deliberate and ultimate rejection of God's loving offer of salvation through His Son.

This is the "abomination of desolation" of which Christ spoke (Matthew 24:15). Those who will then insist on Sunday rest in willful opposition to God's Sabbath will receive the plagues, God's wrath poured out without mixture (see Revelation 14:9-11). In contrast, those who will stubbornly cling to the seventh-day Sabbath will manifest a faith in God that is unshakable.

They will go through the great time of trouble and wash their robes in the blood of the Lamb (see Revelation 7:14).

Because even so many Christians still have confused ideas about salvation, the true nature of the controversy between God's Sabbath and man's Sunday is also not clearly understood. But when the two opposing methods of salvation come clearly into focus, then the true importance of the Sabbath will also be clearly seen. At that time Sabbath keeping will become a test of faith.

At that time, may God give each of us the grace and courage to stand for truth. "He which testifieth these things saith, Surely I come quickly. Amen. Even so, come, Lord Jesus. The grace of our Lord Jesus Christ be with you all" (Revelation 22:20, 21).

Key Points in Chapter 18
The Sabbath Rest

1. The Sabbath is more than a day of physical and mental rest. It is more even than a day of worship. The Sabbath has a redemptive significance, a distinct connection with the gospel.

2. God set aside the Sabbath as a day of rest to signify His perfect and finished work of creation (see Genesis 1:31; 2:1-3; Hebrews 4:4). God rested only when His work was perfect and complete. Adam and Eve, on the other hand, spent their first whole day of life resting on God's Sabbath. Only then did they take up their work.

3. Like creation, salvation begins by resting in the perfect, finished work of Christ—not by doing something.

4. Just as Christ finished creation at the end of the sixth day and rested on the seventh, so He also finished redemption on the cross on the sixth day and rested in the tomb on the seventh day.

5. When sin came into the world, it destroyed God's original significance for Sabbath rest. Humanity rebelled against God and demanded to depend only on self. Mankind introduced his own rest day—Sunday. But his substitute could not point to a finished, perfect work—either of creation or redemption.

6. The final showdown in the great controversy will take place between salvation by faith (symbolized by God's Sabbath) and salvation by works (symbolized by man's Sunday).

7. All who receive the gospel by faith once again enter into God's saving rest, of which the Sabbath is a sign (see Hebrews 4:2, 3; cf. Exodus 31:13; Ezekiel 20:12; Isaiah 58:13, 14).

8. Anyone who is keeping the Sabbath in order to be saved is perverting the very nature of Sabbath rest. If we make Sabbath keeping a requirement for being saved, we are not entering into rest. We are not pointing to a finished, perfect work. We are making the Sabbath into a means of salvation by works—a burden.

9. In the final conflict, the issue will not be between two groups of Christians, or even between two rest days, but between two opposing methods of salvation. The conflict will be

between the seventh-day Sabbath, signifying salvation by faith alone, and Sunday, signifying salvation by human effort.

10. When the two opposing methods of salvation come clearly into focus, the true importance of the Sabbath will also be clearly seen. At that time, Sabbath keeping will become a test of faith.

MARVIN MOORE

The ANTICHRIST and the NEW WORLD ORDER

By the author of
The Crisis of the End Time

Theology is best when it is clear, without prejudice, and seasoned with the grace of Christ. Here's a book that fits the bill.

The Antichrist and the New World Order is a "plain folks" explanation of the end times for non-Adventists. Marvin Moore, author of the bestselling *Crisis of the End Time*, presents the Adventist understanding of the antichrist, America in prophecy, the close of probation, and more in clear, nonjudgmental terms. And, as with *Crisis*, our relationship to Jesus is given top priority.

Whether you have friends or loved ones who aren't Adventist, or you just want an understandable refresher course on end-time events for yourself, **The Antichrist and the New World Order** is the right book at the right time.

Priced for sharing at US$2.95/Cdn$4.00. Paper.

Present Truth in the Real World

by

Jon Paulien

In the ongoing struggle between Christianity and secularism, who's winning? Is the world becoming more like the church, or is it the other way around? How can a church founded in the 1860s compete for the attention of today's secular person?

In this explosive book, Pastor Jon Paulien identifies the task of reaching secular people with the everlasting gospel as the most urgent challenge facing Adventists today. When reading this book, you'll discover:

- Who secular people are and how they think.
- How to meet their felt needs.
- How to live among and work for them without losing your own Christian experience.

This book is too important to pass by. Get yours today!

US$10.95
Cdn$14.80

Available at your local ABC, or call toll free: 1-800-765-6955.